Crystal Healing

for

Animals

By Martin J. Scott

and

Gael Mariani

FINDHORN
Press

First published in 2002

ISBN 1-899171-24-X

British Library Cataloguing-in-Publication Data.
A catalogue record for this book is available from the British Library.

Edited by Lynn Barton
Layout by Pam Bochel
Front cover design by Phoenix Graphics

Printed and bound by WS Bookwell, Finland

Published by

Findhorn Press

305a The Park, Findhorn
Forres IV36 3TE
Scotland
Tel 01309 690582
Fax 01309 690036
e-mail: info@findhornpress.com
findhornpress.com

This book is dedicated

to all the animals

that have helped us

to learn about this wonderful therapy.

DISCLAIMER

Table of Contents

Foreword

By Patty Smith-Verspoor

When *Heilkunst*, the true system of Western medicine, was founded in the late eighteenth century by the German physician, Dr Samuel Hahnemann, he gifted us with the identification of a scientific way of understanding the dynamic nature of disease. This radical act shifted the prevailing concept of disease as something material and chemical to an appreciation for its energetic and dynamic reality. It then follows from this insight that any attempts to influence the state of health or disease of a living being have to be done on the dynamic level for it to be a true restoration of health. To treat otherwise would only palliate or suppress the external manifestations of that internal dis-ease.

The authors of this book have an appreciation of *Heilkunst*, the Healing Art, and have long been doing excellent work in the use of flower essences in helping animals to heal. Now, in this new work, they are sharing with us the ways in which crystals may be used in a new light, enabling us to better discern their action and the role they can play in a true system of medicine based on clear principles. We need these insights so that we can fully develop the use of crystals to benefit our companion animals.

We know that animals are energetic in nature, as are all living beings. However, as easy as it is for us to recognise that they have energetic properties of their own, we often neglect to appreciate that they also have an innate ability to pick up on the energy of others. We see this more obviously when someone comes into the home—if there is no resonance, the animal may do a disappearing act, or show their displeasure in more aggressive ways. If the person visiting is someone with whom they do find a resonant energy, then they tend to stay and ask for attention and affection.

We also need to understand an animal's ability to absorb the energy of the people with whom they share their lives. It is quite common to find that an animal is suffering the dis-ease of the family or of a particular family member. At its most dramatic, animals have taken on the same physical manifestations of disease as their people, including cancer, anxiety disorders, respiratory problems, skin problems and more.

On the pages of this book, where Gael and Martin so ably teach us how to use one of nature's most ancient gifts in the healing of our beloved animals, we are also given the keys to unlock our own insight and powers of discernment. In a natural and wholistic way, these tools will enable us to see more clearly and understand more deeply. We are empowered when we work with our animals on their healing, and help them to lead happier, more productive lives. And in helping our animals to heal, often we are healed as well.

Patty Smith-Verspoor, DVHH, RHom, FHCH, BscEd, is Co-Chair of the Department of Veterinary Studies for the Hahnemann Center for Homeopathy and Heilkunst. She serves on the Board of Directors for the National United Professional Association of Trained Homeopaths (NUPATH) in Canada, and is editor of Heilkunst: the Journal for the Exploration of Hahnemann's Whole Remedial Art. She is co-author, with Rudolf Verspoor, of the ground-breaking book Homeopathy Renewed. She additionally writes for several national and international holistic journals. She lives in Ottawa, Canada, with her three rats, two birds, West Highland White Terrier and quarterhorse filly.

Preface

Many people are surprised when we tell them animals can be treated with crystals. They often seem to think that crystals are only to be used for meditation or other esoteric practices, which may not be of any interest to them. Somehow the idea that you can sit on the floor with a dog and a crystal, or take a crystal out to the stableyard, surprises them: it seems like a clash of two incompatible worlds, the practical and the mystical. It's true that crystals can be used for esoteric purposes, but at the end of the day they are practical healing tools, gifts that Mother Nature has left us to use to enhance our lives and those of anyone we care for.

This book is also a practical tool. It is intended to provide you, the animal enthusiast or caregiver, with a simple yet effective resource that can help you improve the health, vitality, happiness and quality of life of the animals you look after—from a mouse to an elephant and anything in between! Crystals are effective, easily available and generally inexpensive, and anyone can learn to use them.

Everything in nature is deceptively simple, yet for many years crystal healing has remained veiled in myth and magic. The animals do not see it this way. We first became interested in the idea of crystals for animals when our own animals brought crystals into the house, especially one little dog who took a great interest in a particular type of quartzite rock, chose his own pieces from the garden, and had them arranged in his bed at all times. For him, it was the most natural and normal thing in the world. He, among others, taught us that our animal friends are not just aware of the healing resources of our living planet; they are invariably more in tune with them than we are! We dedicate this book to our teachers, the animals. We are only learning; they KNOW.

PART I

Crystal Healing

A Long Historical Tradition

Crystal healing is by no means a New Age phenomenon—far from it! As tools for healing, as religious icons, as philosophical symbols and technological devices, crystals permeate the entire span of human history, forming an undercurrent that unites all societies and cultures across the planet. Crystals are completely fundamental to our daily lives, without most of us even being aware of it.

We know from archaeological records that at least as far back as 25,000 BC, crystals were already drawing human attention in the shape of colourful stones that may have had significance as religious or talismanic objects. Based on what we know of the healing powers of crystals, we can assume that even the earliest and most primitive peoples valued them for their medicinal uses. The Babylonians, the Chinese, the Japanese, the Persians, the Aztecs, the Tibetans, the Aborigines of Australia and the many peoples of Africa, South, Central and North America all used crystals, which also feature heavily in Buddhist, Tantric and Ayurvedic thought. Many of these cultures had, and still have, highly evolved systems of healing involving crystals, both on the physical plane and as "spiritual alchemy" of the soul. Crystals have been venerated in all these cultures, not only for their beauty in art, jewellery and architecture, but also as a key to obtaining enhanced levels of health, vitality and deep attunement to nature. In our own society the deeper qualities of many minerals and gemstones—among them gold, platinum, rubies, diamonds, emeralds and sapphires—continue to be reflected and honoured in the way we prize and treasure them, even though most of us have forgotten their real value.

The ancient Egyptians were very aware of crystal healing as a powerful source of health. Perhaps the most striking example of this is the pyramids, which are said to have originally been capped with crystals and used as a fabulous health-enhancing, life-extending technology, utilising natural healing properties in conjunction with sacred earth geometry. (The great Gothic cathedrals of Europe were built by master masons with this same secret alchemical knowledge derived from the East.) The Ebers Papyrus, dating from 1600 BC, lists medicinal uses for crystals—for instance lapis lazuli and sapphire for cataracts and other diseases of the eye; ruby for liver problems; and emerald for dysentery. From ancient Greece, the work of Theophrastus (372–287 BC) entitled *On Stones* is the earliest example of a formal study of the geological and medicinal properties of stones. Some time later in Rome, the naturalist Pliny the Elder (AD 23–79) produced thirty-seven volumes of writings on the properties of crystals, under the heading *Historia Naturalis.* Then a few years later in the first century AD, Dioscorides wrote his book *De Materia Medica (On Medicines),* a study of two hundred different stones.

Over time, the wisdom of crystals spread throughout the world, intermingled with various other practices such as alchemy and religious worship, and was eventually relegated, like so many things of value, to a diluted and disempowered position outside of mainstream thought. Interest in crystals has flared up from time to time, but it was in the early to mid 1970s that the New Age movement embraced crystal healing and brought about the current resurgence of popularity. Many New Age writers, following the lead of Rudolf Steiner (1861–1925) and others, have made bold and colourful claims regarding the origins of crystal healing in the fabled ancient civilisations of Lemuria (Mu) and Atlantis, which *may* in turn have obtained their fantastically advanced knowledge from alien visitors.

Now, it may be that these societies existed, that the survivors of the destroyed Atlantis were responsible for bringing enlightened thought and technology to ancient Egypt, China and India; or it may not. The fact is we do not really know, and while these legends are thrilling and stimulating to the imagination, whether we choose to believe them is really neither here nor there. Even without hard proof of the mind-blowing wonders of Atlantean crystal technology, we have pretty much enough evidence of the capabilities of crystal healing as a demonstrable down-to-earth tool for attaining health. Slowly, once again, crystals are finding a place in the consciousness of mainstream Western society.

WHAT ARE CRYSTALS?

Crystals form naturally in the earth, whenever conditions allow. When molten minerals and superheated gases from the earth's mantle work their way outwards towards the surface through cracks and fissures, they start to cool. The molecules that make up these substances stop moving about randomly and start to group together into stable patterns. By the time the material has cooled and hardened, the molecules have set themselves into a completely even geometric shape, the most orderly and harmonious possible arrangement, called a *lattice*.

This lattice is the basis of the crystal's structure. Depending on the conditions, or pressure and temperature, at which the crystal was formed and the nature of the liquids and gases from which it was born, the crystal may end up as any one of a huge variety of different types. It may stay in this form for millions of years, or it may grow and change shape, or even metamorphose into different types of crystal if the right conditions arise. But whatever happens, it will always keep its perfectly stable, orderly atomic structure. Even mineral pieces, known as amphorous, that appear on the outside to be without regular shape, for example malachite, have a completely even crystalline structure on the inside. In fact, so even and consistent is the structure of crystals that they can be said to be the most stable and unified matter in the whole universe.

CRYSTAL ENERGIES

But crystals are more than mere atomic structures, however fascinating these structures may be. They also possess some quite remarkable and amazing properties that stretch way beyond the realm of simple matter.

It is well known, even among sceptics and doubters of crystal healing, that crystals have a "charge". This can be easily demonstrated at home by crushing a cube of sugar (which is crystalline, as you can see if you look at it) in a dark room, or by vigorously rubbing two bits of quartz together. The flashes of yellow or green light you see are known as piezo-electricity, and they are caused by the sudden distortion of the crystal lattice, which produces a strong electrical current. The energy flow from a crystal is in keeping with its very regular and even atomic structure. Nothing can equal the absolute regularity and reliability of the electrical pulse they produce. It is for this remarkable electrical property that natural crystals are artificially copied and used in technology. People are often surprised to discover that our modern age of techno-sophistication, which they assume to be purely the product of human cleverness, could not exist without crystals. Since the discovery by scientists that crystals emit a totally stable energy vibration, they have been incorporated as chips into just about every powered item we use, including computers, televisions and watches. Crystals act as perfect, flawless energy transformers, amplifiers and transmitters. Sapphires and rubies are artificially produced and used in cutting-edge technology. The addition of synthetic sapphire to conventional quartz silicon chips has made them resistant to the high levels of radiation found in space or inside nuclear reactors. Laser technology, which allows us to have everything from advanced surgical equipment to CD players and barcodes, is all derived from crystal technology. So are many of the modern toys of the military, including devices that employ laboratory-grown sapphire to confuse and divert enemy missiles, or to steer "intelligent" missiles dead on target with perfect accuracy.

So we are very bound up with crystals in our modern-day technology. But we have focused so much on harnessing the powers of crystals for artificial uses that we have almost entirely forgotten their natural heritage. It's ironic that natural crystals are often used to counteract some of the negative effects of being surrounded by artificial crystal technology, specifically the levels of background radiation we are all constantly absorbing as we enjoy the trappings of modern civilization. This is all somewhat reminiscent of the myths of Atlantis, where it is said the crystal-derived technology became so advanced that Atlantean society was detached from its previously very strong connection to nature, and was ultimately destroyed. Are we to take the legend of Atlantis as a cautionary fable, a prophecy, of what disasters will befall us as a result of one-sidedly embracing the forces of nature for greed, wealth and convenience? That is certainly what we have been doing in the modern age, since the development of petrochemicals and the silicon chip. The most frightening example so far of our perversion of nature is our ability to split the atom and unleash incredible destructive forces. Will our perversion of crystal energy lead to our undoing? Time will tell!

It would have been far healthier for our society to concentrate more on the natural properties of crystals, which were known to the ancients. The real value, and the rightful place, of crystals lies not in their ability to run the computer this book is being typed on. It lies in the realm of healing—in their ability to balance and restore the dynamic functions of mind, body and spirit.

CRYSTALS AND LIFE ENERGY

There is a profound, resonant relationship between crystals and the organic matter of which all life forms on this planet are composed. Most solid matter, including the human and animal body, is crystalline in structure. Quartz crystal is made from silica, which is one of the most common compounds found on earth and an important component of the hair and skin. There is also a high concentration of apatite crystals in our bones and teeth; this crystal is found in the earth and can be used to treat osteoporosis. Crystals are inseparable from what we are. It is very true to say that all forms of life owe their evolution to the mineral kingdom, which is the raw material of all physical bodies. We are all interconnected in this way; this means that crystals have exactly the same significance and the same resonant relationship with us as they have with animals. There is no difference!

When we speak of the resonance that exists between crystals and living bodies such as our own and those of the animals, we are not just talking about the shared way our bodies are made up from crystalline forms. More fundamentally, we are talking about energy, the bioenergy, or natural electricity, that unites us all. Crystal electromagnetic energy, which we have taken from nature and harnessed for our own ends, is exactly the same thing: the natural energy source that emanates from the planet that bore us and governs everything.

We are electrical beings. Every molecule of the human and animal body vibrates at its own electromagnetic, bioenergetic frequency. Like us and all other living beings, animals consist not just of their visible, fleshly bodies but also of invisible energy fields. These fields, which permeate us and surround the material body like an invisible outer shell, are often referred to as the aura, or subtle body.

This book also deals with the chakras. *Chakra* is an ancient Sanskrit word, meaning "wheel", and it refers to the energy centres of the body. It is widely believed that energy enters and flows through the body by means of these centres, which are distributed evenly throughout the body but cannot be perceived by normal senses. Chakras are variously described as rotating vortices, "whirlpools" or funnels. Just imagine them as ports, which draw energy in from the ether to sustain the subtle body. When a chakra is in balance, energy flows freely. When it is imbalanced or closed (or rotating the wrong way, as some people envisage), energy cannot flow properly, and health, either emotional or physical, will suffer. Many natural therapies work on the chakras, as a sort of subtle-energy "surgery". Crystals, too, can be used to balance the flows of energy through the body by rebalancing the chakra system—as we shall be examining later in the book.

The existence and importance of the energetic aspects of the body has been known since ancient times, but research during the course of the twentieth century began to show the first real scientific evidence to back up ancient beliefs. The most striking research came from Russia, with the development of a new type of high-voltage photography by scientists Semyon and Valentina Kirlian in the 1930s. Kirlian photography, which achieved fame a few years ago but is now little talked about despite offering compelling explanations for many unexplained phenomena, shows what appears to be streams and patterns of energy emanating from the physical bodies of humans, animals, plants and minerals. Other scientists, before and since the Kirlians, have described the aura as a biological plasma, or bioplasma, body, forming the unseen yet most vital part of our whole living being. In the 1960s in Japan, Professor Hiroshi Motoyama developed an instrument that is capable of measuring the fields around the body and can detect energy fluctuations in the chakras.

There are actually several layers to the energy body, and understanding it can be quite complex—but for the purposes of this book it is only necessary to understand that living beings are surrounded and permeated with energy. Modern theoretical physics has joined the party, showing very clearly that energy fields are more fundamental to reality than matter, and that one can be converted into the other. Matter is nothing more than crystallised spirit. In other words, the energy fields are primarily responsible for our material form and the condition of each and every cell of the body. Matter is only the reflection, the by-product, of unseen energies, and what we see of the world around us is only the tip of a huge iceberg!

This has gigantic implications for health, because the state of the physical body depends on, and mirrors, the state of the energy body. If our energies are weak, disturbed or out of balance, this disturbance will filter through until sooner or later it will be manifested as emotional and/or physical dis-ease. So sensible (feelable) or visible symptoms of dis-ease are only a physical reflection of disturbances at a deeper, supersensible, or energy, level, and the true source of what we call disease is not carried in matter but in energy. Thus, disease and symptoms are not the same thing. Symptoms are a product of the material world, while disease itself, the progenitor of symptoms, dwells only in the energy, or dynamic, realm. It follows that using chemical drugs, either synthetic or herbal, to remove symptoms can only remove the upper layer of what afflicts us, like pulling a weed but leaving the roots in the soil. *It cannot cure disease.*

Samuel Hahnemann, the genius behind the modern science of homeopathy, recognised two hundred years ago that disease was based in this supersensible world of spiritlike energies and that problems that showed up in the physical body were only expressions of a deeper force that could not be seen or measured. The homeopathic medicines he devised were likewise energetic, or *dynamic* medicines, so dilute that they were essentially non-existent in the physical realm but at the same time very potent for combating disease on the hidden energy level. This is something that only dynamic medicine can do.

DYNAMIC HEALING VERSUS ALLOPATHY

The continuing success of homeopathy and other dynamic healing sciences such as flower essences and, of course, crystals, indicates that these theories must be correct. They are not merely quaint concepts. They work. But to some people, this simple truth is upsetting, perhaps even threatening. From conventional, *allopathic*, medical quarters come scoffing claims that dynamic medicine is worthless, trivial, fanciful nonsense. Because conventional medicine has built its house completely blind to the energy imbalances behind symptoms, believing that disease and symptoms were the same thing, it staunchly (and quite unscientifically, acting more out of emotion than logic) refuses to acknowledge that such unseen imbalances exist. One almost has to feel sorry for allopathy, as it truly has a tiger by the tail: even if it wanted to, allowing itself to embrace dynamic therapies such as homeopathy, flower essences and crystals (and we mean embrace them fully and properly rather than as a dilute and emasculated notion of "complementary medicine") would require admitting that the entire edifice of modern medicine has been built on false beliefs, is fundamentally flawed and needs a drastic rebuild from the ground up. Meanwhile the popularity of dynamic therapies grows year by year amongst a public tired of unnatural and suppressive drug therapies. This poses ever more of a threat to allopathy and its masters, the profit-driven pharmaceutical companies, and so the fear and hatred directed at natural medicine intensify. One of the favourite methods used by allopaths to discredit dynamic medicine is to claim that it operates on "placebo effect"—that is, it has no medicinal powers of its own and acts like faith healing, encouraging superstitious and impressionable folks to delude themselves into getting better. These unfounded attacks are no more than the dying gasps of a way of thinking that is outmoded, scientifically discredited and fit to be consigned to the historical scrapyard. The fact that animals derive benefit from these therapies is an extra nail in the coffin of the allopathic mindset, because even if people can be "fooled" into getting better (and allopathy itself uses placebo remedies), you cannot repeat the trick with an animal!

While modern allopathic drug treatment is limited to working only on the chemistry of the material flesh and the tiny part of reality that we can perceive with our physical senses, energy therapies take a magical, astounding and massively advanced quantum leap into a realm that is as new as it is ancient, as bewilderingly complex as it is beautifully simple. This is where medicine is headed in the future—there is no doubt about it.

TOWARDS A NEW VISION OF THE NATURAL WORLD

As we begin to understand the resonant, harmonious relationship between our material bodies and crystal energy, we come to a whole new awareness of ourselves as part of a living planet. Some scientists have carried this idea even further, suggesting that the actual planet itself *is* a crystal.* James Lovelock, the originator of the Gaia Theory, has famously developed in his books *Gaia* and *The Ages of Gaia* the idea that the planet—the whole planet and everything in it—operates as a single, self-regulating living organism, with its own form of intelligence and perhaps even its own form of consciousness. Lovelock rests this theory purely on scrupulous scientific research, with not a shred of subjectivity or mysticism, and he calls his new science *Geophysiology*.

In this light, could it then be said that crystals are alive, too? Crystals are made of the same matter as we are; they possess an aura; they conduct, absorb and transmit living bioenergy and have the ability to transform unhealthy tissue into healthy tissue. It does not take too great a stretch of the imagination to conclude that, yes, crystals are indeed alive. They are living, immortal, perfect beings. This in turn implies that our understanding of life itself, and what constitutes a living being, is only just scratching at the surface. But as we move forward in our understanding of ourselves, the planet and crystals, we are steadily heading towards a much more enlightened, advanced and healthy vision of the natural world of which you and I are mere microcosms, members of a global community of living beings that takes in plants, animals, minerals and the ether itself.

While these ideas may seem wildly esoteric to some readers, it should be stressed that there is really nothing mystical or strange about any of this, or about crystals or crystal energy. It only *seems* strange because we are suddenly seeing crystals in a new way, not as inanimate lumps of rock or pretty ornaments but as a powerful living force. As Marcel Proust wrote: "The true voyage of discovery consists not in seeking new lands, but in seeing with new eyes."

There should be nothing strange or frightening about working with the natural world. The strange and frightening part is the extent to which we have turned our backs on nature! We personally take the view that crystal energy and healing is as natural as breathing and that

---

* Russian scientists in the 1960s formed the opinion that the earth was formed in the same way as a crystal, growing slowly around a crystalline lattice or a "matrix of cosmic energy". This theory echoes many ancient beliefs.

everyone should be able to make use of it freely and without a second thought. Animals are perfectly aware of what is in crystals, without the need to analyse, theorise or have it proved to them. So let's now move away from the world of theory, and start to look at how these practical healing tools are to be used in the real world.

BUILDING AND CARING FOR YOUR CRYSTAL COLLECTION

A very nice feature of using crystal healing is that it need not cost the earth! Building a collection of useful crystals, perhaps based on the recommendations in this book, can be done very economically. It is not necessary to purchase the large and ornate pieces that are sold in many crystal shops for hundreds or even thousands of pounds or dollars. They are certainly beautiful and very desirable, either as ornaments or for their energetic powers, but for our purposes smaller pieces will do just as well. Small tumbled, or smoothed, pieces are more than adequate for the job, allowing us to build a versatile crystal healing kit that requires little expenditure and takes up little space. (The only precaution with using small pieces of crystal with animals is to ensure they cannot swallow them.) More specialised pieces, such as crystal wands, can cost a little more, but you will only need one or two at most.

So crystal healing will fit any budget. Remember that, with just a little care, crystals will never need replacing. Your crystals will last you a lifetime, forever becoming more attuned to you and more effective in healing. In fact, they will still be there, unchanged, when future civilisations are studying our ancient culture as part of their history education and digging our relics out of the ground.

So let us suppose you have now gone out and started your collection. What next? Crystals are not inanimate objects, and to get the best out of them you need to care for them a little. This is neither difficult nor time-consuming, and establishing a simple routine for caring for crystals will help ensure that you and your animals get the full benefit of their healing powers.

Looking after crystals falls into two basic categories: these are *cleansing* and *charging*.

CLEANSING CRYSTALS

When you first take a new crystal home it is a good idea to wash off any dust or dirt, as it may have been handled by many people or even still have residue left on it from the mining process. Some tumbled pieces may also have glue on them from packaging and methods of presentation, which must be removed. (Do not use detergents, especially with fluorite and malachite.)

Once the piece is externally cleaned, it then needs to be *cleansed.* Cleansing a crystal is a deeper cleaning process than merely washing or wiping its surface, and is very important. The need for cleansing arises because crystals not only transform and direct energy, they also absorb it. The cleansing process rids the crystal of accumulated negative energies which, over time, can come to hamper its effectiveness as a healing tool. A crystal that has sat for weeks or months in a shop may have been near, or handled by, hundreds of people, picking up on all their negative energies: fears, stresses, anger, unhappiness and so on. This may have a cumulative effect on the crystal. We have also found that crystals from certain shops, where the atmosphere was perhaps less positive, needed much more cleansing than ones from other places that were more relaxing and peaceful. A reliable way to check whether your new crystal needs cleansing or not is to dowse over it. (See **Using the Pendulum.**) With a little practice, you will find this becomes a quick and easy routine.

So the initial cleansing is very important. Your crystal should also be cleansed after each healing session, so that it is always ready for instant use.

There are many suggested ways of cleansing crystals, some of them quite elaborate such as cleansing them in wine, burying them in the earth or placing them under pyramids. However, cleansing can be done very simply in every home, and here are some methods for doing it:

1. Holding the crystal over the sink, pour water over it. There is no need to let it sit in the water for any length of time. Then let it dry naturally.*

Beware of cleansing certain crystals with water or salt, as they may be damaged by it. Of the crystals described in this book, cherry opal is fragile and best cleansed by smudging. Boji stone should not be immersed in water, as it may crumble, and malachite and copper should also be kept dry and smudged with incense. Others such as quartzes, moonstone, etc, are fine. But if in doubt, consult the dealer from whom you purchased the crystal.

2. "Smudge" the crystal by holding it for a minute or two in a stream of smoke from sage, cedar, sandalwood, frankincense or cinnamon incense.

3. Spray diluted aromatherapy oils such as bergamot around the crystal, or else burn the oil in a burner and hold the crystal in the smoke as with smudging. (We sometimes buy crystals from a stall that specialises in aromatherapy products, and have found that their crystals never need cleansing when we first bring them home!)

4. Bury the crystal for a day and a night in a container of dry sea salt.*

Once you get used to cleansing your crystals, it can be done very quickly and becomes second nature.

Charging Crystals

To get the best out of crystals, they must be charged, or energised. This is generally done outside. Though it may sound complicated, charging is nothing more than giving the crystal access to an outer source of energy that it can be nourished by. When we get a new crystal, we always cleanse it, removing the negative energy, and then charge it, giving it back some positive energy. It is simply an act of rebalancing the crystal. Charging does not subsequently need to be done each time the crystal is used, but every so often you can give it a charge to keep its energy at its peak.

Charging is quite a personal thing. There are no rules for it, and as you get to know your crystals you will develop an intuitive sense of when they "want" to be charged. Also, the method of charging them is flexible and personal, and the energy you use is mostly up to you. For instance, some people feel that the crackling energy of a thunderstorm provides a great atmosphere for charging crystals, while other people prefer the gentle stillness of a quiet moonlit night. Other times, you may want to charge crystals on a sunny day. Do be careful which crystals you leave out in the sun, though, as certain ones, such as amethyst and rose quartz, can easily fade and lose their colour in sunlight. This will not affect their healing properties, but it would be a

---

*Beware of cleansing certain crystals with water or salt, as they may be damaged by it. Of the crystals described in this book, cherry opal is fragile and best cleansed by smudging. Boji stone should not be immersed in water, as it may crumble, and malachite and copper should also be kept dry and smudged with incense. Others such as quartzes, moonstone, etc, are fine. But if in doubt, consult the dealer from whom you purchased the crystal.

shame to buy a beautiful piece of crystal, only to find it drained of colour! Whatever method you choose, leave the crystals out for at least a couple of hours to gain a good charge. As you go along you will doubtless experiment with different ways of charging different crystals. However, readers who are completely new to this may like to have a pattern to follow, at least initially while they are finding their feet. Our personal approach, which you may like to try out, is as follows:

The more vibrant the colour of the crystal, the more we tend to charge them in the sun. This includes orangey stones like orange calcite, citrine, carnelian and tiger's eye, and reds such as red jasper, ruby, etc. Black stones tend to correspond to the lower chakras and like the vibrancy of the sun, too. The cooler and more delicate colours like fluorite, lapis lazuli and blue lace agate, we prefer to charge in the moonlight in accordance with their cooling and calming attributes. This goes also for delicate greens like chrysoprase and aventurine. Clear quartz can be charged in either sun or moon, but we like to leave them in the sun as we feel that suits their brilliant, sharp energy. Sun and moon can be regarded as the male (commanding, overtly powerful, less subtle) and female (nurturing, gentle and subtle, but no less powerful in her own way) aspects of nature, and this can help to guide you.

However, the best way is to go with your feelings. Look carefully at your crystal. What kind of feeling do you get from it? What quality does it suggest to you? Listen to your intuition on this, and let the crystal "tell" you what it "wants". You cannot really go wrong. Learning how to charge your crystals is not only safe and forgiving, it is also a very pleasurable experience that in itself will bring you closer to nature and the energy of the stones. It is a lovely experience when you get the urge, on a clear night with a full moon, to take all your crystals outside into the garden and leave them in a patch of moonlight. Likewise, it feels very rewarding to let your crystals bask in a warm sun and drink in the rays for a few hours.

When crystals are charged, you may be able to feel their energy as you hold them in your hand. Energy can feel like a pulse or a tingling sensation, like a small electric current. People who are sceptical about crystals are often amazed when you drop one in the palm of their hand and they immediately feel the "buzz" from them!

PART II

Working with Animals

With some theories and understanding under our belt, now it's time to get down to the business of practical crystal healing. **The Crystal Directory** in Part III of this book suggests crystals for healing many of the more common ailments, or areas of trouble, that may affect an animal. Once we have decided what crystal, or combination of crystals, we are going to use, how do we put this into practice?

Let's look first at the most basic way to work with crystals and animals. You have an animal in front of you that needs healing, a crystal in your hand and you want to put the two together! The most basic way to carry out crystal healing on an animal is simply to leave stones in the animal's proximity. This way you are very uninvolved and as long as the animal remains in one spot, the therapy session will practically run itself.

INTRODUCING CRYSTALS TO ANIMALS

Animals often seem to have a conscious affinity with crystals and will sometimes seek them out themselves when they feel a need for them. They appear to sense the energy from crystals more acutely than we do. Some animals will happily accept the healing, while others may take a few days to get used to the crystal energy. For this reason, when it is we who make the decision to use crystals for healing an animal, we should proceed carefully and be sure that at no time are we forcing the energy on the animal against its will. Some therapists consciously "ask permission" of the animal before starting; we personally advocate a more practical approach of "try and see". To start with, kneel down beside the animal, allowing it to feel comfortable in your presence, and once it has settled sweep the crystal, slowly and gently, through the air around its body. Follow the contour of the body, a few inches from the ends of the coat or feathers, perhaps paying more attention to the area that needs healing. Often you will get some reaction from the animal as the crystal passes through the energy field of the affected area. If the animal seems happy to remain close to the crystal, you can then place others around it in whichever way desired, and retreat to a distance to let the stones do their work.

If the animal seems uncomfortable, shifts around or walks away, do not press the issue. Try again later, and build up the short sessions until you are able to keep the crystal in the animal's energy field for longer periods. Eventually, even resistant animals will usually feel quite comfortable with the crystals. If the animal persistently walks away from a particular crystal, it may be a good idea to try using another type. Perhaps the animal is trying to tell you something!

PLACING THE CRYSTALS

Working with animals is highly rewarding but often presents problems of its own. With humans, it is (normally) easy to get your patients to co-operate and stay still while you place crystals around them. Animals can pose quite a challenge! Probably the easiest ones to work with in this way are dogs, who are often quite happy to laze about co-operatively while you place stones around them. Even a boisterous youngster will eventually settle down and let you do your stuff! Cats are in second place, and will often settle on sofas and armchairs in the home so that you can place crystals around them. Luckily, cats and dogs are the most common pets. Certain other animals, such as pigs, will also allow themselves to be surrounded by crystals.

Horses and ponies present specific practical problems. For a start, they are very seldom lying down, and even when they do lie down they very often jump to their feet as we approach. This makes it hard to leave crystals around them. There is also a safety issue in laying crystals around a horse, as it may easily tramp on a sharp piece and do damage to the frog, or soft part of the underside of the hoof. Crystals would also be likely to be crushed, pressed deep into the ground or lost in the straw. Some people have described to us how they sew terminated (pointed) pieces of quartz into the inside of their horse's rug, making it possible to fit the rug on the animal's back and have the crystals held in place. Although this is a good idea in theory, in practice a horse may injure itself if it lies down or rolls on the ground. So with horses, it is generally advisable to stay with them during the session, and hold the crystal or crystals in place manually. The large size of these animals can mean having to enlist a friend to help, if more than one crystal is going to be used at a time.

When it comes to birds, rodents and fish, it is hard to place crystals with any degree of accuracy, and the best policy is just to leave the stone somewhere near the animal. The healing energy will still reach its mark. As long as the crystal is able to be immersed in water and is nontoxic (check beforehand), a piece could be placed in a fish's tank. Tumbled, rounded pieces are best for safety (don't use jagged or sharp crystals) and always ensure that the pieces are large enough that the animal won't swallow them! A practical tip with aquariums and cages: if you obtain crystal pieces that have been prepared as jewellery and pierced to accept a string or chain, you can dangle the crystal in the water or in the cage on the end of a thread. This makes it easy to pull out again without opening cages and having escaped rats or canaries running loose in the house, or having to plunge your arm in amongst the fishes!

Assuming that it's practical to be accurate in the positioning of the crystals, how do you know where to put them? This depends on the nature of the problem being treated. Crystals affect the whole energy field of an animal, but placing them at certain points of the body will focus the energy more strongly on one spot. For instance, a thyroid or respiratory problem that is located around the neck or throat will often respond well to a crystal placed in that area. If you can, place the crystal near the spot you wish to heal. If you can't, don't worry too much.

Another way of placing the crystals is by setting them out in organised layouts. A number of these are described in the section **Healing Layouts for Animals.** Alternatively, you may wish to go by the chakra system. (See **Chakras and Chakra Balancing**.)

Often, after about fifteen minutes, the animal will get up and walk away, indicating that it has had enough healing for now and the session is over. Fifteen to twenty minutes is quite long enough for a session in any case, so do not chase the animal around with the crystals if it has shown you it no longer needs them. Be patient, and wait until the animal accepts them once more. One session a day is fine. Remember, crystals are powerful tools. This is the reason we are cautious about the advice given in many books, namely that crystals can be attached permanently or semi-permanently to an animal's collar. Although we sometimes advise this ourselves, we urge that the crystal should not be left in place for too long, or be forgotten about and the animal left unsupervised. It is wrong to force the animal into the crystal's energy, or to take away its ability to move away from the crystal if it wants to.

CRYSTAL MASSAGE

There are two basic forms of crystal massage. One involves using proper massage techniques, along with oils, and lies outside the scope of this book. The other type of crystal massage, which we will look at here, is simpler to use and does not require any knowledge of normal massage techniques. It does not even involve touching the animal! This kind of crystal massage is a very effective procedure that has many uses: it can help to aid and speed up healing of wounds, sprains, and so on; it can help to ease pain and reduce discomfort; it is relaxing to both humans and animals and has an overall energising effect on the whole body.

As this technique brings the healer into more intense contact with the crystal energy, some people may need a bit of "grounding" before starting. Being grounded simply means that you are focused on what you are doing, and that you are protected from picking up on any negative energies from a sick animal. Lack of grounding can occasionally make healers tired, nervous and slightly disorientated. Many practitioners of natural therapies, as well as psychotherapists, complain of feeling exhausted at the end of a day of treating people. These therapists would benefit from grounding and protection. There are different methods of achieving the necessary focus and stability— burning candles, using aromatherapy oils, walking in bare feet, or eating chocolate! Carrying a grounding stone that will work on the base chakra, for instance hematite or black tourmaline (which also protects against negative energies), is an effective way of doing the same thing with crystals. These stones could be worn in a pendant or carried in a pocket, or you could take the essence.

To carry out the massage, you will also need a wand. This inevitably conjures up images of wizardry and Harry Potter novels! But a massage wand in crystal healing is simply a long (generally no longer than about five or six inches) piece of crystal, often artificially cut from a larger piece which enables wands to be made from any kind of crystal. Clear quartz is a good wand for general massage purposes. Massage wands are pointed at one end and rounded and smoothed at the other, for a special reason.

Once you are suitably grounded yourself, your wand is well cleansed and your animal patient is settled and calm, you are ready to start. Take the wand in whichever hand feels most comfortable, and hold it with the rounded end pointed at the animal, pointy end facing outwards away from the animal. There is a reason for this—the wand is a directional device and will absorb energy and send it in a particular direction. Energy always flows from the rounded end out of the pointed end. What we are doing here is drawing negative energies out of the animal's aura and sending it outwards into the ether. You may feel you do not want the pointed end aimed straight at your own body. Many practitioners feel that to protect themselves from any negativity flowing out of the patient, they like to point a finger of their free hand downwards to send any transmitted negative energy to earth, where it is safely absorbed.

Hold the end of the wand three to four inches from the animal's body. Starting at the tail end of the animal's body, move the wand in small *anti-clockwise* circles as you slowly work your way up towards the head. Remember that you are not contacting the animal's physical body, but are acting directly on its energy body. We liken the anti-clockwise motion to "unscrewing" the negativity out of the animal. As you are doing this you may run into "knotted" areas, areas of blockage and difficulty. You may have the feeling that while the crystal was previously running smoothly through the animal's energy field, it suddenly comes to a place where it feels as though it is being dragged through treacle or thick mud. This produces an unmistakable heavy feeling, and indicates that the area needs more work on it. Concentrate on the area until you feel that the crystal is dragging less. Bear in mind that more work will be done in future sessions, and that you do not have to spend hours! Just keep a note of the sticky areas, and monitor their progress from session to session.

When you reach the head of the animal, the wand now needs to be turned to point in the opposite direction, with the point now facing towards the animal and the rounded end facing you. You are now going to work your way back down the animal's body, this time using small *clockwise* movements, basically doing the exact opposite of the previous procedure. Where before you were removing negative energies from the animal, now you are bringing a fresh charge of positive energy back into the animal. We like to think of the clockwise movement here as "screwing" positive energy back in. This dual process of first cleansing out negativity and then introducing positivity is a direct echo of the process of cleansing and charging a crystal.

Work your way back down the animal's body the same way you came up, in a mirror image of the first process. Some practitioners like to have a finger of their free hand pointing upwards at this stage, to conduct energies downwards through themselves and into the animal via the crystal. When you have finished, let the animal stay still if it wishes, or wander off at its leisure. You may notice that the animal seems very relaxed and will go off to sleep. This is quite common and perfectly normal; indeed it's often a very good sign that the treatment has made a difference, especially if it marks a contrast to the way the animal was beforehand. If, however, you see no difference in the animal, this does not necessarily mean the treatment has failed to work. Every contact the animal has with crystals does it nothing but good. Depending on the animal and the problem being treated, it may take a few sessions before a difference is seen.

You yourself may like to drink a cup of tea or coffee and take a few minutes to relax after the massage session. If you have grounded yourself properly beforehand you should not feel dazed or excessively sleepy—but if you do, please take the time to come out of it and waken up fully before recommencing your normal activities.

LIQUID CRYSTAL ESSENCES

Crystal essences have many uses and are of great importance as a healing tool. A crystal essence, sometimes given the name elixir, has exactly the same healing properties as the substance of the crystal from which it is derived, and so it is interchangeable with the actual crystal. Essences utilise the ability of water to record and store the energy signature of the stone in the same way that homeopathic remedies and flower essences do. As in the sun method used for flower essences, the rays of the sun are used to potentise the healing energies of the crystal and transfer them into the water, which then forms the basis for the liquid remedy. Thus, the essence contains none of the material substance of the stone, just as a flower essence contains none of the material substance of a flower; essences are pure energy, the living healing power of a natural substance extracted and kept bottled ready for immediate use.

Let's look at some of the possible advantages of using a crystal essence rather than the stone itself:

1. Several essences can be combined together in one handy bottle, which can be carried anywhere ready for use at a second's notice. This is often far more practical than having a pocketful of different crystals that may drop out and get lost. An essence treatment bottle contains only a few drops of crystal stock essence (see **Making Your Own Essence**) and costs little to replace if it is lost or smashed.

2. Crystals like gold, ruby, and emerald are expensive to buy and perhaps not always suited to the rough-and-tumble of animal healing. Essences can be bought ready-made, so one can leave the job of obtaining pieces of precious stone or metal to the essence producer!

3. Using essences means not having to introduce the animal to the crystal, which can save time especially if the animal is hard to work with, or in emergency situations where it is far easier to administer the liquid by dropping or rubbing it into the animal's mouth or skin.

4. When animals are aggressive and/or extremely fearful and cannot be approached, any kind of contact therapy, including crystal healing or hands-on healing methods like TTouch, Reiki or acupuncture, may be completely impossible. In these instances, which happen fairly often when working with distressed or suffering animals, traumatised animals in rescue homes, or wild animals, essences can often be added to the animals' food or drinking water without having to enter their enclosure. It is also effective to add a few drops of essence to a water-filled spray bottle and mist the essences around the animal from a safe distance. Sceptics may consider that this way the essence will be too dispelled in the air to have any effect; but, in fact, we ourselves have had astonishing results using crystal essence sprays on unapproachable animals, sometimes bringing about a complete change in just a few minutes.

5. Essences can be used in creams or added to oils for massage therapy, adding an extra healing dimension to any treatment.

6. They can be mixed into other liquid treatments, for example into flower essence treatment bottles, homeopathic "wet" doses, and so on.

7. It is possible to treat more than one animal at a time from the same bottle, cutting down on time, expense and manpower. This makes essences ideal for kennels, zoos or any situation where several animals need treatment.

Essences are very convenient for easy daily use, and can be added to food or water, rubbed into the skin or coat topically, added to creams, oils and sprays, or given straight from the bottle, although care must be taken with animals in case they bite off or swallow the glass dropper tube, which could be extremely hazardous. They are often recommended by practitioners for use in between regular crystal layout sessions, to maintain the healing influence consistently. It is, of course, completely impossible to overdose with crystal essences, just as with flower essences. No possible harm can occur from giving a few extra doses, such as in acute or emergency situations.

Crystal essences are generally very easy to make up at home. However, some crystals can be difficult or awkward to make into essences, such as boji stone, or contain toxic elements that must not be transferred into the essence for oral use (copper, malachite).

Any crystal essence can be purchased ready made from suppliers listed at the end of this book, and we would especially recommend this if you have never made essences before, or in the case of fragile or toxic stones.

Tip: *Beginners at essence making could start with crystals from the quartz family—stones such as clear quartz, rose quartz, milky quartz, aventurine, amethyst, bloodstone, carnelian, citrine and chrysoprase. That way they can be assured of absolute safety and will not harm the crystals. If possible, use tumbled stones that will not splinter and leave shards in the water.*

MAKING YOUR OWN ESSENCES

To make your own crystal essences, follow this procedure:

- Take a clean, sterilised, clear glass jug or bowl.

- Put the chosen crystal into the vessel and fill it up with spring or mineral water (still rather than gassy). Before doing this, always ensure that your chosen crystal is suitable for immersion in water.

- Cover with a muslin cloth or a jelly-bag to prevent dust or dirt from getting into the water.

- Place the vessel in direct sunlight outside in as clean, quiet and natural an environment as you can find—not by the side of a busy road!—where it should sit undisturbed for at least two hours.

- After this, carefully strain the charged liquid into a bottle or bottles (depending on quantity). We would recommend the use of rubber bulb-type dropper bottles, which can be purchased as empties.

- Add approximately 30 to 50 per cent brandy to the bottle or bottles to act as a preservative (for the water rather than for the energy). These bottles are now your *mother essence.* To make a *stock bottle,* add two drops of mother essence to a dropper bottle filled with brandy. The stock bottle, so-called, is the form in which you would normally buy an essence from a supplier. Drops can be taken from the stock bottle (or indeed the mother essence bottle) but it is possible to dilute the essence another stage to make a *treatment bottle.* Simply add 2 drops from the stock bottle into a further bottle containing approximately 70 per cent spring water and 30 per cent brandy. Several different essences can be combined in one treatment bottle, to make up an individualised daily treatment for any animal or person. When the essences have been added to the treatment bottle, give it a light tap or a shake to mix it up and energise the contents.

- The normal dose from the treatment bottle is 4 drops, four times daily. When adding to feed it is often better to give 8 drops, twice daily, for no other reason but that this tends to fit in better with animals' mealtimes. The effect is no different, but you should be aware that crystal and flower essences work best when given regularly and repeatedly at fixed and frequent intervals. It basically does not matter how essence drops are given: in water, snacks, or even dropped on the palm of your hand and licked off by the animal.

- The same essence may be added to a spray bottle and used to spray around the animal, taking care to avoid eyes and other sensitive areas. As mentioned, sprays are ideal when animals cannot or will not be approached.

- A mother essence bottle can go a very long way, producing hundreds of stock bottles and thousands of treatment bottles. However, should you run out of mother essence, the same piece of crystal may be used time and time again to produce literally unlimited quantities of essence. This is in contrast to flower essence-making, where the body of the flower is sacrificed so that its spirit can be perfected and immortalised.

It is often said that essences should be stored away from electrical equipment and strong-smelling substances like mint and perfumes, in case they might be corrupted. In our understanding of the matter, essences may be composed of subtle energy, but this certainly does not mean they are in any way delicate; and it is unclear exactly how this "corruption" could happen. As far as we are concerned, very careful storage of essences is not of prime importance. But certainly it will not do them any harm, either!

At the end of the **Crystal Directory** in Part III are listed a collection of suggested combination crystal essences, which you could easily make up yourself from individual essences, or have made up for you. These combinations are designed to cover a wide variety of healing needs common to animals of all types, ages, shapes and sizes.

USING THE PENDULUM

The pendulum is a tool that has many uses, and it is worth developing skill with it. The practice of using the pendulum is called dowsing, and it is the art of connecting with our intuitive side in order to access information from the unconscious. The unconscious is a much deeper thing than our own mind, and deeper even than the idea of the "collective unconscious" proposed by the psychologist Carl Gustav Jung. It is a vast pool of thought, intuition, energy and information that unites all living beings and all of nature, encompassing the human, animal, plant and mineral kingdoms, plus all of the dimensions that cannot be seen or felt. Being able to tap into it allows us stunning insights into things we could never consciously know. The pendulum gives us access to an enormous bank of knowledge, but it cannot say anything on its own and can only respond to a question or stimulus. When asked a question, it has three responses: YES, NO and DON'T KNOW. These responses come from us ourselves, or more correctly, via us, as hologrammatic microcosms of the wholeness of nature and the universe around us, and the pendulum is only reflecting, or translating, them as signals we can see and recognise.

Always ask the pendulum simple questions, where the answer is to be YES or NO. For example, don't ask: *"Is my animal sick and should I give it rose quartz?"* Ask each question separately. *"Is this animal sick?"* YES... *"Does it need rose quartz?"* NO... or whatever is the pendulum's answer. Try also to ask objective questions. *"Will I win the lottery this week?"* is unlikely to gain an accurate response (something called wishful thinking!).

Many people believe that using crystals (and flower essences) over a period of time helps us to develop the intuitive side of ourselves allowing us to make contact with a deeper world through the pendulum. Indeed, some long-time users of energy therapies are astounding pendulum dowsers. The ultimate development of this skill is seen in people with strong telepathic and divining abilities.

The best pendulum to start practising with is a plain wooden one, with neutral properties. The uses of the pendulum include

1. Choosing crystals to purchase (Ask: *"Is this crystal right for me?"*)

2. Selecting crystals or crystal essences for healing, either for yourself or another person or animal

3. Determining whether or not a crystal needs cleansing and/or charging

4. Checking the condition of the chakras* and the overall state of health

5. Running checks by distance, or using a chakra chart*

Once you have obtained a pendulum that feels good for you, if you have never used one before, do not try to achieve complete mastery of it in the first day! This will be counterproductive and lead to frustration. The whole key is to relax and not try too hard. Make some time for yourself, and retreat to a quiet place where you will not be disturbed. You may wish to start by grounding yourself or spending a few moments in gentle meditation or relaxation. Then take the pendulum, holding it by its string and letting it dangle two to three inches from your fingertips.

You need to understand the signals the pendulum is giving you, so the first step is to clarify what they mean. Relax, do not consciously move your hand, and say (either in your head or out loud): *"Give me a YES"*. Do not force the pendulum to move, but simply wait for the unconscious forces in your own energy field to act upon it. At this point, hopefully, you will see it start to swing. Don't worry if the movement is very slight, as you will improve with time. YES is very often a clockwise motion.

When you have practised awhile and are sure of your YES responses, try the NOs. It is the same procedure: *"Show me a NO"*. Many people get an anti-clockwise motion for NO, while others say theirs is a left-right swing, like a shaking of the head.

If the pendulum seems to hesitate, gives a poor response or does nothing at all, this probably indicates a DON'T KNOW, which may mean your question is inappropriate or needs rephrasing.

Before any session with the pendulum, it is advisable always to check the YES and NO responses. It is rather like zeroing a scale and ensures that you always understand the signals the pendulum is giving you. With time and skill, you may become so confident in the feel of the pendulum that you are able to dispense with this ritual; many practitioners have amazing attunement with their pendulums and go straight in without any preparation. As with anything, this will only come with patient practice.

Very often it's possible to choose crystals and other natural remedies for animals purely based on logical choice, matching the animal's symptoms or problems to the proven, documented qualities of a particular stone/essence/remedy. Other times, however, we may be less

---

*See **Chakras and Chakra Balancing**

sure what to give an animal, and we need guidance. This is where the pendulum is very useful, like an oracle we can query when in doubt. Always be careful, however, not to allow your subjective preferences to override the natural response of the pendulum.

To select crystals or crystal essences for an animal, have a row of crystals or essence bottles in front of you. If the animal is not present, try to bring it into your mind and connect with it. You want to build a bridge, or a connection, between the energy of the animal and that of the crystals. The pendulum is like a meter that connects the circuit and gives you a gauged response. Hold the pendulum with one hand, relaxed as usual, and with the other hand try placing a finger on each crystal or essence bottle in turn, waiting for the response of the pendulum. It may select, say, three or four out of ten crystals, and you can then look these up to reinforce your intuitive choice. If using actual stones, you can then ask where they need to be placed on or near the animal, using a chakra chart. (See **Chakras and Chakra Balancing.**) For each chakra, place your finger on a colour and wait for the response. Dowsing over an actual animal (or person) is the same procedure: with the patient settled and still, work your way from the base chakra upwards, holding the pendulum over the animal's body or putting your finger on the chakra.

It is possible to dowse through literally hundreds of crystals or essences in just a few minutes. Practitioners often keep their essences in kit boxes, perhaps ten or twelve bottles to a box. They start by dowsing over the boxes themselves. If they get a NO, they know to lay the whole box to one side. If the pendulum says YES, they will dowse over each individual essence in turn and place the chosen ones together. Once the pendulum has made its selection, it is then up to the practitioner to decide how to structure the treatment, which essences should be given first and so on. The pendulum can also be used for this fine-tuning. Many practitioners actually depend entirely on the pendulum in their work, and find it gives them completely reliable and consistent information. The dowsing process works exactly the same when using actual crystals.

There is a simple beauty to working with the pendulum. There really is no mystery to it, although many people initially find the concepts very overwhelming and hard to swallow. Once you start to use it, you will start to regard the pendulum as a real friend.

Chakras and Chakra Balancing

In Part I we looked at the idea of the chakras, the invisible ports through which energy travels to sustain the aura and the physical body. Chakras can be overactive, that is, too open, letting through too much energy; or they can be underactive, or closed, not letting in enough energy. Hyperactive behaviour would be an example of what may result from chakra overactivity (here it would be the base chakra, and if the base chakra was underactive, this could lead to lethargy and fatigue). If you look up some of the crystals that resonate with the base chakra, you will see that ruby, bloodstone and hematite can all be used (to a greater or lesser degree) to treat either hyperactivity or lethargy. All healing crystals have the ability to regulate and rebalance the flow of energy through a certain chakra or combination of chakras. Chakra balancing, where crystals are used to work on several chakras at the same time that are out of balance, is an excellent way of helping to maintain general health. As with any exercise regime or healthy diet, you don't have to wait for the animal to be ill to do a chakra balance.

In humans there are seven main chakras. Some people claim that animals have fewer—or, absurdly, none at all! We personally feel that there is no reason why animals should not have the same number of chakras as we do. They respond well to chakra layouts; dowsing over their chakras with a pendulum gives clear results; and apart from anything else, our intuition tells us that we too are animals and have much in common with our furry, feathery or scaly friends. Without a heart chakra, an animal could not love—and they do. Many animals show unconditional love that is greater than that of humans. Without a throat chakra, an animal could not express itself—and they do! For the purposes of this book we are going to assume the same seven major chakras exist in an animal's subtle anatomy as in a human's. This may be thought by some readers to be excessively anthropomorphic. But we believe that when we know how to interpret animals and read their higher emotional and spiritual qualities through their behaviour, it becomes clear that there is really little difference between their species and our own.

The seven chakras are laid out as follows:

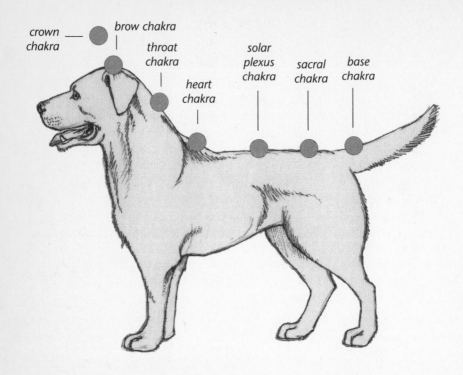

crown chakra

brow chakra

throat chakra

heart chakra

solar plexus chakra

sacral chakra

base chakra

At each chakra point, energy passes right through the auric and physical bodies, permeating the entire organism. Working along the dog from the tail to the head, we have

1. The base chakra, traditionally represented as red. This is situated at the base of the spine, where it meets the tail, and corresponds to the adrenal glands, motivation and energy. The will to survive and to reproduce are rooted in this chakra.

2. The sacral chakra, traditionally represented as orange. This corresponds to the reproductive system, sexual drive and function.

3. The solar plexus chakra, traditionally represented as yellow. This corresponds to the liver, pancreas, stomach and nervous system.

4. The heart chakra, traditionally represented as green. This is to do with love and hate; compassion—or lack of it—for others; resentment and loyalty; and, on the physical level, lung-related problems such as asthma.

5. The throat chakra, traditionally represented as light blue. This governs the energies of the thyroid gland, the throat itself and the neck area. The throat chakra is also linked to communication and personal expression, how we interpret and relate to the world about us.

6. The brow chakra, traditionally represented as dark blue. It is associated with perception and insight (such as telepathy), and emotional aspects such as fears. Physical resonance is with the ears, nose, left eye and nervous system.

7. The crown chakra, traditionally represented as lavender. The crown corresponds to spirituality in humans (in animals this translates into their harmony with nature), and to connection with cosmic energies. On the physical level, it is linked to the right eye and pineal gland. Function of the pineal gland is relatively little documented in the conventional literature of Western medicine, simply because so little is known about it (some textbooks do not even bother mentioning it). It is more highly regarded in Eastern medicine. Jan de Vries, the world-renowned naturopath, describes it as "the aerial to cosmic energy", which when disturbed can affect the entire body. Animals, living much closer to nature, have a larger and better developed pineal gland than humans.

A note on the colours associated with the chakras:

> chakras themselves have no colour. However, through the ages each one has come to be linked and identified with a particular colour. The field of colour healing shows that colours themselves have particular energy vibrations and can have an effect on the physical body. The colours attributed to the chakras may be seen as symbolic, but ancient wisdom suggests that they are more than that.

Chakra balancing is simply a question of laying out different crystals along the length of the animal. For the base chakra, choose a crystal that resonates with it; for the sacral, choose one that resonates with that, and so on all the way up the line. Choosing between different crystals that resonate with a given chakra will allow you to fine-tune the chakra balancing to the individual animal. The **Crystals and Chakras Table** in the Appendix shows at a glance which crystals resonate with which chakras.

Balancing the chakras with a generally healthy animal is, as we have said, not something that needs doing very often. Animals are usually better balanced than we are!

What might need doing more often is balancing individual chakras that are out of balance in a less-than-healthy animal. It is possible to determine which chakras are out of balance using the pendulum, and you should find that what the pendulum tells you corresponds to the illnesses of the animal. For example, as you work your way up the chakras of an animal with a kidney problem, the pendulum will indicate a NO in the region of the sacral chakra. An animal that has been abused and traumatised may indicate a NO in the region of the heart chakra. And an animal that is very low in energy will often indicate a partial closing of the base chakra. Then, from the data you have gleaned, you can make a choice of crystals to rebalance energies wherever necessary.

USING A CHAKRA CHART

The same results may be obtained using a multi-coloured chakra chart, which you can make up at home with coloured marker pens.

The chart can be any shape desired, perhaps a semicircle or a round pie chart. In the example shown, the colours run from the base upwards, left to right; but this is not vital. To operate the chart, first connect with the animal in your intuitive mind, imagining the animal and stretching out to it with your thoughts and feelings. When working at a distance, it often helps to have a photo of the animal or a cutting of hair to act as a "witness". With the pendulum in one hand, run a finger of the other hand across each colour in turn, noting the response of the pendulum. With a little practice you should find that the pendulum's YES and NO replies are the same with the chart as they are when dowsing over the actual animal. In this way, it is possible to run a chakra check whenever needed, adjusting the crystal prescription accordingly.

USING CRYSTALS FOR RESCUED OR ABUSED ANIMALS

Unfortunately many animals receive a bad deal at the hands of humans. The lucky ones wind up in animal sanctuaries and rescue centres, where they have a chance of finding a new home. Giving a home to an animal that has suffered in the past is a very generous and praiseworthy act. But sadly, very often, people underestimate the potential difficulties involved in rehoming a rescued animal that may have suffered from extreme trauma and abuse. In some cases, the horrors that these animals have been through can only be guessed at, and they are so marked by the experience that even the most caring and loving owners find it hard to form a rapport with them. These animals often end up back in the sanctuaries, and while they are well looked after, they miss out on what they most need in life—a loving relationship in a family.

If at all possible, once you have decided you would like to adopt a particular animal, be it a cat, dog, pony, donkey, rabbit or hamster, try to find out as much as you can from the sanctuary staff and/or previous owners about the animal's past history. Many animals will have a known past, but others will be more of a mystery and their past experiences can only be guessed at through their behaviour. Watch for fears, nervousness, aggressive tendencies, self-mutilation of any kind and any sort of unpredictable behaviour. And try to be sure that if you are going to take this animal on, you will be able to cope with it. Then make your final decision.

Any animal, and particularly one with a difficult past, needs help to settle into its new home. When you bring your adopted animal home for the first time, it may be rather bewildered and overwhelmed. This is where you can start with crystals or essences right away. **Smokey quartz** will have a calming effect and helps animals adapt to changes in their circumstances. On the physical plane, it would be very suited to animals that suffer from stress-related diarrhoea. **Jadeite jade** also helps the animal that is stressed by a sudden change, especially if it shows signs of fearful aggression. Remember that nearly all animal aggression towards humans is based on fear. Punishing it, either physically or verbally, is absolutely not a viable cure for the animal's problem.

We feel strongly that any rescued animal, or any animal with a difficult past, whether or not it has spent time in and out of sanctuaries, should be treated for emotional traumas, *whether these are known or unknown*. Traumas include frights, beatings or chronic states of fear or suffering. Perhaps the animal was starved; or perhaps it lived in perpetual terror of a particular person who always mistreated it. As you get to know your rescue animal better, you may see the signs: a horse that is terrified of the sight of a tall man, or of a stick, or of a rope, is giving you an insight into things that have happened in its past. A dog that cringes or urinates in submission when you casually raise your hand to scratch your head or reach for your coffee cup is putting out definite messages that it hasn't forgotten its unpleasant past. Animals have long memories. We know a mature adult Great Dane that is quite confident until she sees a hosepipe. Then, she acts fearful because she remembers the neighbour who used to cruelly dowse her with cold water over the fence when she was little. Another dog we worked with was consistently afraid of the sight of a blue leash, but not of a red one— which leads us to imagine that the animal associates the blue leash with a past traumatic incident such as being tied up or beaten with it. Just like people, animals can become phobic and respond to sights, sounds, even smells that trigger their memories. Crystal therapy offers them the chance to release these locked-in, fearful, toxic memories, so they can return to a more normal life. With its wonderful flexibility and safety, crystal therapy allows us also to make educated guesses about the past life of an animal and base our treatment on supposition, in the knowledge that if we are wrong, the treatment will do no harm.

Aventurine is an important crystal, or crystal essence, for healing the retained "fingerprint" of past abuse that will otherwise not fade with age and will be triggered again and again. If the animal is showing signs of distress to the point of defensive aggression, especially towards one particular person (usually a man, hinting at past beatings from another man), use **rose quartz**. This is an extremely important crystal to use in these cases. An animal that has been badly treated by our kind cannot be blamed for expecting more of the same sort of treatment when it sees another human approaching. How is it to know that our intentions are kind and caring? What would you do in that situation—would you not lash out? Rose quartz is excellent for easing resentment and hatred that may have stored up in the animal's heart (closing the heart chakra) during the hard times in its life. The remedy helps animals let go of their fear and anger and develop the capacity for trust. **Gold** would be a useful addition to rose quartz in this context, and will actually enhance any essence or essences with which it is given.

Another key crystal to use with many rescue animals is **hematite**. This will help the animal that has been traumatised and is showing signs of poor vitality. In that way it is similar to the Bach Flower Essence **Wild Rose**, which helps animals that have become apathetic and disinterested. The crystal or essence will have an uplifting effect on the animal's emotional state but also have a greater impact on the physical body, boosting energy and helping assimilation of iron.

If you inherit or adopt an animal that may have been traumatised, and it later becomes ill, take it to the vet for treatment in the usual manner but do not discount the possibility that the events in its past are likely to be at least partly responsible for the development of the physical condition. We all know that chronic stress weakens our immunity to disease and can even trigger cancer. The same is true of animals, and treating for the past trauma alongside whatever other treatment is used will help recovery.

Many animals end up in sanctuaries and rescue centres because they have come from dysfunctional, often violent homes. They will have witnessed all manner of arguments and rows, unhappy people yelling and screaming and hurting one another, or people acting in a frightening and unpredictable manner because of alcohol or drug abuse. As we have said, the animal does not forget these experiences, and an animal that has witnessed such unpleasantness will get very upset at rows and emotional outbursts in your home, even if they only happen occasionally. Any stresses, marital discord, family problems, rifts and disputes will also have an effect on the animal. Now, ideally we should be able to avoid these situations in our family lives! But every home does have its tensions. Placing an **amethyst** cluster in the main family room of the home can help to create a more harmonious and peaceful atmosphere. And for the animal that appears stressed by our own emotional lows—the so-called sponge effect—a very effective crystal is **black tourmaline**. It could be used alongside any of the other crystals for past abuse/trauma, and will assist in the healing of the emotional wounds by protecting the animal from negative stimuli in the present.

USING CRYSTALS IN ANIMAL TRAINING

Crystals have an important role to play in the training of animals, either in the formative education of young animals or in reshaping undesirable behaviours. Although crystals, like flower essences, are still relatively unknown to trainers, they are highly effective in this field, and it is hoped that their use will become more common in years to come.

To start with, what do we mean by training? The word sometimes conjures up images of strict, inflexible regimes, the animal equivalent of boot-camp! For the purposes of this book, training takes place whenever we have to teach an animal how to act, for whatever reasons. Many animals learn things instinctively, but there are times when they have to be shown. Training, then, covers anything from teaching a horse to go into a trailer for the first time to teaching a goat not to barge for his food; from litter-training a cat to carrying out advanced obedience or police training with a dog. Whatever we attempt to undertake, the backbone of all good training is bonding, trust, patience, mutual communication and focus. All of these qualities can be obtained and enhanced using crystals.

PRE-TRAINING

Before you even start training an animal, be it a new puppy or a young horse, it is important to build up a good rapport with it. Many people acquire animals that are fearful or traumatised, or that simply have not been properly socialised. Launching straight into training with an animal like this will prove fruitless and may even do more harm than good. It is possible to do a lot of constructive work using games and play, but the use of crystals will enhance the process greatly.

If an animal acts fearful or appears to be very sensitive and nervy, before starting any training it would be a good idea to try using **aventurine**. This crystal or essence will help with nervousness under stress as well as with any traumas in the animal's past. It is not necessary to have detailed knowledge of the trauma, or even to be 100 per cent sure that there has been one! But if a frightening or traumatic incident has left any imprint on the animal's mind in the course of its life, use of this essence over a few weeks will help alleviate it.

In addition, both the animal and the trainer will benefit from using **boji stone** and **herkimer diamond** in conjunction on a regular basis, to help form a strong bond between them and amplify two-way intuitive communication. This can be given regardless of whether the animal is fearful or not, and can make a real difference to the progress you make together once training actually begins.

THE TRAINING PROCESS

There are quite a few crystals that will help with different problems and barriers in the training process. **Ametrine** is useful for many young animals that may act in a scatty, hyperactive manner and display a very short attention span. **Carnelian** would be useful here too, and also where the animal seems to be "dreamy" and "not with it". Some animals, particularly young animals such as the puppy at his first training class, may feel very overwhelmed by the many things going on around them, and may show confusion and lack of mental focus. The crystal to help with this, and other cases of sensory overload, is **citrine**.

Amethyst can additionally be brought in for the animal that is hot-headed, wild and temperamental, such as a spirited young colt or an adolescent dog that perhaps measures himself against you. This is effective in many cases of mild mutiny or non-co-operation, but you may also need to address your hierarchical relationship with the animal. More simply put, it's not a good idea to let big animals walk all over us! If you think you have a budding or established dominance problem, whereby an animal is attempting to impose its leadership upon you by displays of force or intimidation, or is generally very stubborn and appears to view your training efforts with contempt, try using the crystal **platinum**. If things have degenerated this far, though, you have stepped out of the training arena and will have to redress the relationship between you and the animal before you can come back to training.

A popular idea that has come into training is the idea of left/right brain. This approach is now being used by well-known animal trainers, such as the equine trainer Pat Parelli. In his highly successful Natural Horse•Man•Ship education program, Parelli states:

> There are two terms I like to use to describe the thinking condition of a horse: left brain and right brain. When horses are "left brain" they are using the thinking side of their brain. They are calm, in a learning frame of mind, and can think their way through situations and requests. When they are "right brain" they are not thinking, they are reacting on instinct. They are usually in the flight or fight survival mode, where there is no time to think.

Horses, as "flight" animals, are indeed very right brain by nature. But so are dogs, the other species we tend to focus on for training. Dogs are predators rather than prey animals—but they are just as prone to falling into an unthinking, distracted and unco-ordinated mode of behaviour during training. An excellent balancer of left and right brain characteristics for all animals in training is **fluorite**. An animal whose attention is divided and scattered, who has trouble retaining lessons and starts losing concentration through mental overload, can be helped to refocus its mind and think more clearly about what it has been requested to do. We have used this essence to teach retrieve skills in a very short time to a young dog that previously could not comprehend what was being asked of him and would just give up and lie down. Interestingly, this crystal is said to raise the IQ!

Another very useful essence in balancing left and right brain is **malachite,** especially in combination with **ruby**. We discovered this when we treated a four-year-old Quarterhorse after a trauma. Montana, as he is called, had got stuck in a barbed wire fence and suffered severe emotional scarring despite not being physically injured. We had treated and alleviated the trauma using a flower/crystal essence combination that happened to contain both ruby and malachite. When he was fully recovered, Sandra, his owner, recommended training him. She still had some of the essence combo left, and discovered by chance that when she gave a few drops to Montana at the start of a training day he would be more focused and confident. She found he absorbed his lessons faster and seemed to be thinking more and acting more logically. Sandra reported this back to us, and we were curious to pinpoint the elements within the combination that were having this effect, as the essence had not been originally intended as a training aid. On investigation, we realised that it was the two crystal essences in the combo, ruby and malachite, that were enhancing the horse's training. We then gave just these two essences alone to a client of ours who was having trouble training her dog. She gave them to the dog and the effect was replicated. Since then, we have used the combination many times, often together with **fluorite** when extra co-ordination is needed for detailed and precise training such as agility and dressage. The positive effects that can be got by balancing the right and left brain confirm the findings of Pat Parelli and others.

EXPOSURE TO RAYS AND RADIATION

This is an area of animal therapy that is often neglected. Yet animals, and the humans they live with, are often subjected to powerful, unnatural influences that may reduce their vitality or even make them very ill. These influences are acting on us every day, all the time, without our knowledge. So what are they, and what can we do about it?

One of the worst environmental toxins we have to deal with is rays and radiation. Our modern age of manufactured power brings us material comfort and convenience. It brings us electricity on tap, around which our whole lives revolve. It brings us microwave ovens that miraculously save us the bother of actually cooking food ourselves. It brings us cell phones that allow us to send e-mail messages from the back of a taxi. The world we have built up around our endless and bountiful sources of artificial energy seems incredibly enriched and wonderful. We are benefiting from it at this very moment, using the convenient medium of a PC to type these words.

Yet there is an extreme price to pay, and we are all paying it. For we poison ourselves every day and potentially ruin our health, that of our children and that of our animals, with toxic levels of background radiation.

Now, we tend to think of radiation as something that only becomes a problem after a nuclear blast, when levels go through the roof. But, in fact, consistent exposure to radiation from TVs, computers, smoke detectors, cell phones and all the other electrical equipment in the home, as well as higher levels outside the home from broadcasting towers, weather forecasting devices, microwave towers, large power lines and transformers, medical X-rays, and so on, not to mention emission from nuclear power stations and weapon testing, all builds up to present a major threat to health.

We are told all the time (usually by parties with a vested interest) that the levels of radiation involved are safe, that when they fall below a set level there is nothing to fear. But who sets these levels? The truth is that there is no such thing as a safe level of radiation. We, and our animals, inside and outside the home, are suffering damage to our health right now as a result of these unseen forces. The excellent book *Radiation* by John Davidson is a detailed and scientific account of exactly what this radiation is, where it comes from and how it affects us.

The veterinary surgeon Dr Richard Pitcairn is one of the few animal experts to lay stress on this issue, and he writes about it extensively in his book *Natural Health for Dogs and Cats* (co-written with Susan Hubble Pitcairn). The Pitcairns stress that owners of any animal suffering from epilepsy, blood disorders, behavioural disturbances or any sort of cancer should consider the possibility that radiation in one form or another is very likely to be an exciting factor or possibly even the cause. Further examples of radiation-related health problems they cite are: genetic problems such as birth defects and mutations; "physiological interferences" that cause changes in the blood cells, hormonal and biochemical processes; physical ailments such as headaches, low energy, hair and feather loss, cataracts, loss of co-ordination and balance, and senility.

In recent studies, scientists in North Carolina exposed samples of human blood to low-level cell phone radiation and consistently found that a genetic change occurred, the blood developing high levels of cells containing micronuclei. Cancer experts regard levels of micronuclei as a diagnostic marker for high cancer risk. (It is precisely these micronuclei that scientists were looking for in the aftermath of the Chernobyl disaster in 1986; they tested the blood of children living near the power station, and those who showed high levels were considered to be at a greatly increased risk of developing cancer.) Another study in St Louis has shown that cell phone radiation produced micronuclei in mouse tissue.

Experiments carried out on the effects on animals of ELF (Extremely Low Frequency) energy fields, such as those that surround high voltage power lines and carry for thousands of feet in all directions around them, have yielded more frightening results. The Pitcairns write that:

> *[ELF fields] have been found to:*
> * *Influence chemical balances in the blood of rats*
> * *Slow down the heartbeat of salmon and eels*
> * *Interfere with the ability of homing pigeons to find their way home*
> * *Cause changes in hormones, stunted growth and other signs of chronic stress in mice*
> * *Cause bees to cease storing honey and pollen, to kill each other and abandon or seal off their hives (causing death by asphyxiation).*

The example of the bees makes for a disturbing parallel with human societies. It makes us wonder what kind of a world we have created. In the context of the evolution of the planet, it has taken humankind just the blink of an eye to wreak havoc on the natural environment and the innocent animal kingdom, purely for financial gain and convenience. Clearly it is going to take a major revolution of thought before significant changes take place to reverse this trend on a global scale. But in the meantime, what can we do as individuals, to help protect our own health and that of the animals we have unwittingly dragged into this unnatural situation?

In our own experience of working with animals, we have come across the problem of radiation toxicity, both inside and outside the home. Two of the case studies at the end of this book show how animals were deeply affected by the problem of background radiation, and how crystals were able to help deal with the negative effects. Crystals are part of the solution to this problem.

A number of the crystals described in this book, as well as many others, offer protection from the destructive energies of radiation. They do this by enhancing the electromagnetic capacities of the physical and subtle bodies. All of the quartz family, including clear and **rose quartz, amethyst, citrine,** and many others, can help to protect against all types of radiation. Leaving pieces of **quartz, malachite** or **black tourmaline** near computers and television sets lessens the adverse effects of their emitted radiation.

Many crystals stimulate the immune system; a strong immune system also aids to protect against such negative outside influences and makes it harder for them to trigger disease states and miasms (inherited predispositions to certain diseases). **Citrine, clear quartz** and **gold** are particularly useful in this regard. Another hazard to animals, this time to ones that have already fallen ill or been injured, is the use of radiation in conventional veterinary treatment. Obviously, sometimes it is definitely necessary to use the X-ray machine to check for broken bones, foreign bodies, growths and tumours. But every time an animal is X-rayed it is receiving a significant dose of toxic radiation that will remain in the system forever and accumulate. The other most common source of exposure to radiation in veterinary treatment is radiation therapy for serious illnesses such as cancer. Rose quartz and citrine specifically help protect against radium, making these essences useful for any animal or person who is to undergo a medical X-ray.

A useful crystal and flower essence combination to help offset any biological damage that animals may suffer when exposed to such sources of radiation, would be

Crystal essences:
> **Black tourmaline**
> **Citrine**
> **Clear quartz**
> **Malachite**
> **Rose quartz**

Flower essences:
> • **Yarrow Special Formula** (consisting of **Yarrow**, **Arnica** and **Echinacea** essences) from **FES, California,**
>
> **OR**
>
> • **Electro Essence** (consisting of **Bush Fuchsia**, **Crowea, Fringed Violet, Mulla Mulla, Paw Paw** and **Waratah** essences) from **Australian Bush Flower Essences**
> (Flower essence formulas available from IFER—See Appendix for address.)

*Method: mix 4 drops of each crystal and flower essence into a 30ml treatment bottle (see **Making Your Own Essences**) and give 4 drops, four or five times daily until contents are used up.*

Some people may like to follow these ideas for further back-up treatment:

• **Radium** in homeopathic potency, 30c*
• Combination of all twelve tissue salts (Bioplasma) in one, for example Dr Reckeweg. This cell replacement therapy, not strictly homeopathic, may be given over a period of time to build the vital force.*

HEALING LAYOUTS FOR ANIMALS

Some of the following are adapted from the work of Sue and Simon Lilly, and we have found them to work as well on animals as they do on people. Position the crystals as shown. These drawings are not to scale!

---

* You may like to contact a professional homeopath or homeopathic vet for guidance on dosage of homeopathic remedies and tissue salts.

1. THE AMETHYST LAYOUT

This requires eight amethyst pieces of more or less the same size, which are arranged as shown. If using terminated pieces, place with the points facing inwards, pointing towards the animal.

This layout
- Brings about relaxation
- Helps with stress and anxiety
- Quietens the mind and soothes the nerves

2. THE MOONSTONE LAYOUT

This layout requires five pieces of moonstone. Lay out around the animal as illustrated.

The moonstone layout is good for
- Blockages in the sacral and solar plexus chakras
- Hormonal imbalances
- Problems relating to the digestive system and abdominal region

3. The Smokey Quartz Layout

The smokey quartz layout requires twelve terminated smokey quartz pieces, laid out with points facing outwards.

This layout
- Helps the healing process
- Helps with any recent shocks or traumas
- Removes toxins

4. The Black Tourmaline Layout

Eight pieces of black tourmaline are needed for this layout. They are laid out as two crosses, one aligned with the top, bottom, right and left of the animal and the other rotated around a few degrees clockwise.

This will help to
- Clear up aches and sprains in the muscles
- Protect against emotional negativity (sponge effect)
- Rebalance the skeletal structure (almost like a form of "crystal osteopathy")
- Relax the body generally

5. THE CLEAR QUARTZ TRIANGLE LAYOUT

This simple layout requires only three clear quartz points, laid out as shown. It can also be focused on individual parts of the body, for example a paw. The layout can be placed around an animal's bed at night to aid recovery from illness and give the vital force a boost (provided the animal accepts the energies).

The clear quartz layout acts
- To boost energy in the whole organism
- To heal injured parts

6. THE ROSE QUARTZ LAYOUT

Twelve small or tumbled rose quartz pieces of roughly similar size are needed for this layout.

This layout is good for
- Aggression and fear in an animal
- Effects of past traumas and abuse

It would be more effective to use the rose quartz layout after the worst of the negative emotions have been treated with crystal essences.

Part III

Crystal Directory

The Crystal Directory is the heart of this book. It starts with an alphabetical guide to thirty common and readily available crystals. These crystals will form the basis of an excellent all-round therapy kit for every owner or carer of an animal. For each crystal the following information is given:

- An at-a-glance summary of the crystal's uses in healing mental/emotional, behavioural or physical problems, where applicable. For each crystal, this section is divided into two parts: **Healing Qualities**, indicating the positive healing attributes and capabilities of the crystal, and **Indications for Use**, showing the negative states of emotional and physical dis-ease that the crystal can be used to heal.

- An indication of the relationship of the crystal to the chakras, or energy centres, of the body.

- A brief physical description of the crystal. This will help readers to identify stones in their collection more easily.

- Specific information on the treatment of a variety of domestic and wild animals, based on research carried out by the authors and other therapists and writers.

- References to other sections of this book that offer further detailed guidance on specific issues.

Following the alphabetical guide is a list of common ailments and problems met in animals, covering the mental/emotional, behavioural and physical levels. Use it to quickly track down crystals for treating a particular condition. Then consult the entries in the guide for the relevant crystals.

Finally, there is a collection of six suggested crystal essence combinations that could be used for a range of specific purposes. It would be a simple matter for the animal carer to make up these combinations from individual ready-made essences.

GUIDE TO CRYSTALS

AMBER	
Healing Qualities	Absorbs and dispels negative energy Aids healing process on many levels Boosts immunity to illness Calms and sooths Detoxifies and purifies Revitalises, strengthens and protects
Indications for Use	Aging Allergies Arthritis and Rheumatism Asthma Bladder problems Colds Depression Digestive Infections Intestinal problems Poor healing Respiratory problems
Chakra Resonance	Solar Plexus, Throat

Technically speaking, amber is not a crystal but rather an organic substance. Anyone who has seen the movie *Jurassic Park* will know that amber is fossilised tree sap. It can be yellow, red, brown or even green in colour, but is more usually an amber colour, as the name would imply.

Amber is a stone with diverse healing properties. It pervades the whole organism and helps to boost healing on many levels. Through the ages it has come to be regarded as a protective, detoxifying and purifying substance, capable of absorbing and dispelling negative energy in the physical and mental/emotional realms. On the physical level, it thus allows for greater resistance to allergens, infections, colds, and bronchial and asthmatic conditions. This makes amber a very useful and important crystal all year round but especially in the wintertime, when animals—particularly those with lowered immunity, perhaps due to age or other illnesses—are often open to infection. Other conditions often associated with winter and older animals, such as rheumatic pains and stiffness, can also be helped with Amber. The crystal will help to draw out the pain.

The protective influence of amber extends to healing intestinal upsets, very common in dogs, and bladder troubles, such as cystitis, very common in cats. These types of ailments can be helped by placing a piece of amber near the affected area (it could be sewn into a little pouch attached to the collar of any animal that is prone to such conditions) or by using the essence, either given orally in food or water, or gently massaged into the fur. Amber will help to soothe the animal's discomfort, bringing relaxation and quiet.

On the mental and emotional levels, amber acts in the same protective, purifying kind of way. It has been used to help soothe depression in humans and animals, and will assist in bringing about a greater sense of calm and positivity.

Regular use of amber, either the stone or the essence, will help revitalise and strengthen the whole system.

AMETHYST	
Healing Qualities	Eases the pain of losing or being apart from a loved one Serves as a general calming stone Helps in training young, hot-headed animals Soothes fears and stresses
Indications for Use	Bereavement and grief Disorientation Fear Panic attacks Pining Separation anxiety Training problems
Chakra Resonance	Brow, Crown

Amethyst is a very commonly used crystal and an important member of your crystal collection, both as a stone and as an essence. It is a member of the quartz family and is violet to deep purple in colour. Some amethyst beds are spectacularly beautiful! But beware of leaving amethyst out in the sun, as it may lose its colour. This one is best charged by moonlight.

Amethyst helps with grief after losing a loved one. As anyone knows who has lived with animals and shared painful experiences with them, they as well as humans experience pain at bereavement—sometimes even more acutely than we do. Whether it is a human family member who has died or one of the animals in the family, everyone suffers. Therefore using amethyst at such sad times will help all. (See **Case Histories: Toby, Joanne and Cleo**.)

Losing a loved one does not always have to involve the loved one's death. When animals are separated from their friends, companions and carers for whatever reason, they may undergo a high degree of emotional stress, or what we would term *grief* in human emotions, and using the stone or the essence will soothe them and help them to survive the inevitable sad period after the loss without losing too much vitality or succumbing to illness. Thus amethyst is a key crystal in the treatment of separation anxiety in any animal that has been suffering from being kept apart from its carers and companions. The classic example of this is the pet that has had to spend time in a kennel or cattery or quarantine pen, pining for its owner. There have been many examples of previously symptom-free animals falling seriously ill and even dying after periods of enforced separation. Stress is a very destructive force for animals as well as humans, for what it does is lower the vitality of the whole system, open the doors to invading agents of infection such as bacteria and parasites, and, more seriously, offer a cue for the triggering of latent miasms, or pre-set, inherited tendencies to particular diseases, which may manifest in unpredictable ways as anything from skin problems to cancer. Another crystal that offers support after a loss or separation and that helps to protect the lowered system against falling ill, is r**uby**.

In human treatment, amethyst is commonly used to treat insomnia and nightmares. In working with animals, we have found that elderly or ill animals, who perhaps feel quite threatened, lonely, fearful and vulnerable when left on their own at night, can be helped with this crystal. We treated an elderly dog that was suffering from panic attacks and disorientation at night. Leaving a piece of amethyst near his bed helped ensure that he slept soundly and unperturbed.

Amethyst is a good stone to have in the home, to act as a general calming influence. A good idea might be to place a medium-sized cluster in a central position in a family room such as a living room. As well as being an attractive ornament, if the crystal is regularly cleansed and charged it will help dispel a lot of the ambient negativity that affects everyone in the house, human and animal.

Amethyst may also be used in training hot-headed animals such as wild and temperamental young colts. (See **Using Crystals in Animal Training**.)

AMETRINE	
Healing Qualities	Balances excessive or depleted energy levels Helps animals know "when to stop" Soothes agitation Uplifts and revitalises
Indications for Use	Depression Fatigue and exhaustion Hyperactivity Hypersexuality Low energy Nervousness Training problems Uncontrollable behaviour
Chakra Resonance	Solar Plexus, Brow, Crown

Also a member of the quartz family, this unusual crystal is a combination of **citrine** and **amethyst,** and has the properties and colours of both. It is effective when given to young animals that display signs of hyperactivity, for instance a young puppy that has overdone it playing with children or other dogs, and is uncontrollably "hyper" despite being exhausted and needing rest. On the other hand, because it resonates with the Solar Plexus chakra, it is able to boost energy and produce an uplifting effect in a tired, listless or depressed animal.

Sheepdogs such as Border Collies and German Shepherd dogs often display an abundance of energy which sometimes stands in the way of their training or may even render them uncontrollably nervy. If the problem is not due to boredom, a lack of exercise or inappropriate diet, such animals can benefit from ametrine to help calm them down and make them realise when it is "time to stop". Ametrine can, in fact, be combined in essence form with the Bach Flower Remedy **Vervain**, to great effect. We have named this hybrid essence "Vervatrine", and use it a great deal in our work with hyperactive, hard-to-train animals. (See **Using Crystals in Animal Training**.)

With states of apparent hyperactivity, do check that the hyperactive behaviour is not related to diet. Certain foods may simply be inappropriate for certain animals, depending on their type, age and levels of exercise, and if behavioural problems are linked to dietary issues, you will find that your crystal therapy can do little to help!

Working backwards, if you find that a hyperactive or "crazy" animal is not responding at all to therapy, diet is one of the things to consider next. Similarly, if the animal calms down with the crystals, you know that the diet is not the problem.

Sexual arousal can also lead to states of hyperactivity that may be so powerful as to cause distress in an animal. We have used both ametrine and "Vervatrine" with very good results to calm a Pekingese dog who was driven insane with longing each time his companion Spaniel bitch came into season; as he was denied contact with her, it sometimes looked as though the unfortunate Peke were about to have a heart attack! After a few drops of the essence, the little dog would start to settle, and after three or four doses would eventually go off to sleep. Obviously, one should not rely entirely on ametrine to guard against the call of nature, and it should not be seen as a substitute for keeping dogs apart during season-time, or for having them neutered if necessary. But there may be times when ametrine will need to be called in to take the edge of such extreme states of agitation.

AVENTURINE	
Healing Qualities	Boosts resistance to stressful situations Can be used in massage Heals emotional scars Lends confidence Soothes fears
Indications for Use	Fear Nerves under stress Oversensitivity Past abuse Rescue animals Show nerves
Chakra Resonance	Heart

Another quartz, this mostly pale, cool green crystal is strongly indicated for various emotional problems in animals, with the accent on fear and nervousness. It is particularly good for very sensitive and nervy animals that take fright easily or appear distressed for no apparent reason. This can often be the case with so-called prey animals such as rabbits and horses. The natural instinct of a prey animal is to be constantly on guard against predators, and while this is a positive survival instinct, in some cases it can render an animal oversensitive to the slightest thing. Flighty, highly bred horses such as thoroughbreds can prove a real handful when they act in a jittery way, either during riding or general handling, and their spooking at everything that moves can pose a real danger when out on the road. Aventurine is one of the key crystals that can help to bring about a greater sense of calm and confidence in these horses. It would also be of benefit to their nervous riders, as often the horse itself is not out of balance but is only reacting in typical horse fashion to the nervousness it perceives in its rider. In the herd, all members look to the leader for moral support; if the leader appears afraid, that indicates to the others that it's time to panic! If the leader appears calm and unworried, the others get the message that all is OK. Thus, if we are to be a responsible and firm herd leader—which we must be with horses, if we are to have a positive rapport with them and avoid potential problems of bullying and biting, it is important to be quite calm and relaxed. Many problems that riders experience would be significantly eased if both horse and rider used this crystal.

Certain canine breeds including Greyhounds and some Spaniels can also be quite prone to nervousness, and this can be a problem for people who wish to display their pet at shows. Nervousness in the show-ring is a guarantee of failure, and it is distressing for owners to see their animals in a nervous state. If Aventurine essence is given to the animal each day for two or three weeks before the event (though this may be much longer than necessary) it can help to reduce nervous agitation very considerably. As with horses and riders, it would be a good idea for owners of show animals to share the essence with their pet, as animals are experts at picking up on our own anxieties. The influence of aventurine allows us to be placed in stressful situations without being overly affected by them.

Some animals do not just inherit their nervous tendencies, but develop them as a result of trauma, suffering and poor treatment. Any animal that has come into your home from an animal sanctuary or rescue centre, or who may have a difficult past would benefit from this crystal even if the details of the traumas it may have experienced are unknown. This property of aventurine in healing past traumas unfortunately makes it a very commonly used crystal, as so many animals are marked by cruel treatment at the hands of previous owners. While some animals seem to bounce back quite well once they are relocated to a more loving environment, other animals that are particularly emotionally sensitive such as horses and certain dog breeds, will never recover unless offered some sort of treatment. Horses have extremely long memories and will remember traumas and beatings all their lives. Many Greyhounds, cast-offs from the lucrative racing industry, are traumatised for life when callous owners abandon them roughly and heartlessly. For these types of situation, consider aventurine to help heal these unseen, yet very deep, wounds.

For information on how to spot an animal that has been treated with abuse or cruelty, see the section on **Using Crystals for Rescued or Abused Animals**.

To build up a really close and trusting relationship with a rescued or previously abused animal, try using aventurine essence mixed in a lotion as a massage treatment. Many animals respond brilliantly to touch therapy, and this method offers the added qualities of the crystal. Any light non-greasy oil, such as sweet almond or golden jojoba, will do as a carrier oil for this technique.

BLACK TOURMALINE	
Healing Qualities	Balances and regulates hormonal levels Helps animals adapt to being brought into the human environment Protects against background radiation Protects animals against humans' emotional negativity Realigns the physical body Undoes damage caused by stress
Indications for Use	Hormone imbalances Muscle strains and pains Radiation Skeletal problems Sponge effect Stress from human contact
Chakra Resonance	Base

There are different coloured tourmalines, but this one is jet black. It is also known as schorl. This stone gives excellent protection for an animal that is prone to picking up on its owners' negativity. This is especially necessary for animals that spend a lot of time in human company, such as those domestic animals like cats and dogs, birds and rodents that live with us in our homes. When animals pick up on or mirror the negative emotional states of their keepers and owners, absorbing and holding negative energy, they are suffering from what is know as the "sponge effect".

Another category of animals which benefits from black tourmaline are wild animals that have not been used to human contact and are suddenly brought into the human world, for example zoo animals. We have to realise that we humans carry with us a great deal of stress and negativity, and while we think we can cope with it, to animals it represents a very powerful and noticeable negative force. Many animals will fall ill or lose vitality if exposed to it for too long.

Andrea Freixida is a biologist and flower essence practitioner living and working in Sao Paulo, Brazil. She has her own clinic called BioFauna, and is also associated with the Park Ecological de Tiete in Sao Paulo where wild animals are taken to be rehabilitated for release into the jungle after having been captured for the exotic pet trade. Many of them have been abandoned. Andrea uses black tourmaline a great deal in helping these animals to overcome their experience of human contact. It has proved so useful, in fact, that she and Steve Johnson, founder of AFEP, the Alaskan Flower Essence Project (which incorporates gem and crystal essences) have included it in a dynamic essence combination called **Animal Rescue Formula.**

Black tourmaline is also one of the main remedies for the negative effects of background radiation from computers and other electrical equipment (See also **Malachite**). This crystal, either the stone itself or the essence, is ideal protection for small caged animals such as hamsters, guinea pigs, mice and birds that may live within radiation fields and cannot get away from the source of the problem.

We all know that a soothing massage after a hard day at work is an ideal way to dispel stress that has built up in the body, making shoulders tense and sometimes causing backache. Emotional stress and muscular/skeletal problems often go together. This points to another property of black tourmaline, which is its ability to work on the physical level to ease many problems of tension that have become lodged in the body. Using pieces of black tourmaline in a layout around a person or animal can help to relieve all sorts of stiffness and pains. It appears to have the ability to realign the skeletal structure—a lady we treated, who had needed frequent and regular manipulations from an osteopath for a ligament problem in her inner thigh, experienced a complete and, so far, permanent recovery after a few black tourmaline layouts. The same healing quality applies just as well to animals, and any animal that suffers from stiffness and pain in the limbs may very well benefit from black tourmaline. Especially if this stiffness and pain appears in the animal following a trauma or period of stress, or if the animal is having to suffer living in the home with you during periods of family turmoil such as frequent arguments, marital rifts, serious financial worries, and so on—then think of black tourmaline for its ability to work on both the physical manifestation and the emotional cause. Animals so often act as mirrors, showing us where we are going wrong. This is a good thing, but the animals can suffer as part of the process, and we really do have a responsibility to return the help they give us!

(See **Black Tourmaline Layout** for more information on how to use the stones.)

Another physical healing quality of black tourmaline is its ability to help balance and regulate hormonal levels. Hormonal imbalances can affect animals when overwhelming stress knocks their whole system out of balance; this crystal will help to right the emotional imbalance caused by the stress, and the physical hormone imbalance may well right itself as a knock-on effect. We would venture to say that just about any physical problem in animals and pets may be indirectly triggered by stress and the sponge effect; and so black tourmaline could be brought into use as part of just about any treatment, for any disease.

It is also known that exposure to levels of background radiation can have an adverse effect on hormonal balance. Black tourmaline, in helping to protect against such radiation, also offers a balancing influence on the hormones. If your animal is diagnosed with a hormonal imbalance, using this stone may well help as part of the treatment of the condition, particularly if the animal lives indoors with you and may have been sleeping or spending time close to VCRs, computers and other radiation-emitting equipment.

BLOODSTONE	
Healing Qualities	Aids and supports the internal organs Boosts energy Detoxifies liver, kidneys and spleen Increases overall strength and vitality Purifies the blood Resonates with blood disorders
Indications for Use	Acute and chronic laminitis Anaemia Animals coming out of hibernation Bleeding wounds Blood disorders Constipation Convalescence Fatigue and exhaustion Heatstroke Kidney problems (consult vet) Poor circulation Toxicity
Chakra Resonance	Base, Heart

As its name would suggest, this stone has a strong affinity with the blood. This is reflected in its appearance: it is a greenish stone with red spots that look very like drops of blood.

Bloodstone is a very important crystal that aids and supports the workings of many vital organs and acts as a cleanser and detox remedy. It helps with general healing, increases the strength of the whole organism and assists with both resistance to illness and recovery from it. Animals that are convalescing from disease benefit enormously from the cleansing, refreshing and energy-boosting properties of bloodstone. Also, if they have been subject to a lot of drug medication in the course of their illness, they will need something to help dislodge the toxic material from their organs. This is an added benefit of bloodstone. We would recommend bloodstone, either in stone form or as an essence, for any convalescing animal.

Conditions where an animal appears exhausted, lethargic or lacking in energy, can be helped with bloodstone once you are certain that the animal is not ill. In the summertime, unwary animals that get caught in the sun too long and suffer from heatstroke can be treated with the crystal. If this happens, bathe the animal with lavish amounts of water that has had a few drops of bloodstone essence added to it. The last time we had to do this was for our white drake Jehovah, who strayed too far from his pond on a very hot day and was seen zigzagging drunkenly with heatstroke. Bloodstone had a very rapid effect on him.

Bloodstone works with the blood in a number of ways: it helps to prevent and to heal anaemia, it has been used traditionally to help stem the flow of blood from wounds, and it will help to rebalance any condition of the blood that causes poor clotting or healing. As a cleanser and purifier of the blood, it has been brought into use in the treatment of leukaemia.

Bloodstone can help as a treatment for acute and chronic laminitis in horses. The stone's effect on blood circulation also plays a part in healing this condition, improving the flow of blood to the feet and strengthening the liver. For horses and ponies prone to this condition, it would be a good idea to add bloodstone essence to feed each day for a few weeks prior to the danger season in spring, when the grass is at its most lush. Note—this is not a cure for laminitis, which is a serious and sometimes fatal disease! The suggestion here is to be used as part of a preventative programme of good horse management.

We generally recommend bloodstone for animals that have taken a lot of conventional medicine, especially antibiotics, or have been exposed to pesticides such as flea sprays and other toxic treatments. The essence may be added to animals' drinking water as a periodic detox treatment and to support the liver and kidneys. Another useful trick is to leave a bloodstone overnight in water (preferably still mineral or filtered water). Next day, remove the stone and use the water as drinking water for pets. This is good to do on a very hot day, as the water will then act as an energising drink for them.

Because of its ability to support tired or weakened systems and get things moving and flowing again, bloodstone has been used to help give a boost to animals that seem to be slow in coming out of hibernation. The crystal was used in the case of a hedgehog that was found in a country lane one spring. The hedgehog seemed to be still half asleep, and was so extremely lethargic that he could barely drag himself along the ground. The person who found him was concerned he might be ill, and so had him checked by a vet. Nothing was found to be wrong with him, and bloodstone was used to revitalise him. Within a couple of days, the hedgehog was wide awake and happy to be released back into the wild, scuttling energetically off into the bushes. A vet of our acquaintance has used bloodstone to help treat a pet tortoise that also seemed to be having difficulty coming out of its winter hibernation. The bloodstone provided that little extra boost that allowed it to awaken from its long sleep and become more active— insofar as a tortoise can actually be said to be active!

Bloodstone is also useful for straightforward cases of constipation. Obviously if the constipation is severe and long-lasting, see your vet as it could mark a serious condition. But in simple cases, use the essence added to drinking water. Constipation will often be eased within a day or two.

BLUE LACE AGATE	
Healing Qualities	Calms vocal and demanding animals Cools and calms Soothes inflammation and heat of the body and mind
Indications for Use	Anger Attention-seeking animals Bites and stings Females in heat Fevers Grumpiness and bad tempers Inflammation Tired, inflamed eyes
Chakra Resonance	Throat

Blue lace agate is a cooling and soothing stone of a delicate striated sky blue. The look of the stone suggests calmness and tranquillity, detachment from irritation and annoyance, and a state of mind that is relaxed and pleasant. In keeping with its appearance, blue lace agate does indeed serve to engender a sense of peace and calmness in those that use it. It is very useful for calming down states of anger, whether an acute flare-up in the face of some stressful or annoying incident, or a more deep-seated and chronic state. An animal that displays a grumpy tendency or always seems in a bad mood, may very likely be helped by this crystal. Of course, it may be worth investigating *why* the animal is like this, as it may also be due to fear, insecurity or an unresolved past trauma.

The keynote to blue lace agate is heat. Anywhere there is heat, whether in the emotions or in the physical body, blue lace agate can be used to quell and soothe. It neutralises "red" energies, the energy of heat, fire and passion. The word *inflammation* literally means "on fire", and so any part of the body that is inflamed can be helped to heal itself with this stone. For instance, a sting, if the skin around it is hot and inflamed, can be soothed with topical application of the essence or even just application of a piece of the stone itself.

Fevers and high temperatures may also be helped with blue lace agate, although we would urge an animal's carer to check with the vet that a temperature is not a sign of something more serious.

Tired, inflamed eyes, quite often seen in old dogs, can be treated using a cool compress that has had a few drops of blue lace agate essence added to it. As well as soothing the heat and irritation of the eyes, it will help calm the animal's mental agitation and frustration.

Female animals in season, or as it is commonly described, "in heat", may also be helped by blue lace agate to lessen their nervous, agitated behaviour. Heated emotions may also cause demanding, obsessive and attention-seeking behaviour in animals. Sometimes this is also related to training, for example a dog that has been "taught" to demand attention because he is always given a pat on the head or a stroke for his efforts. These sorts of problems are often solved simply by being more aware of the way the animal responds to us. However, imbalances in the throat chakra may lead an animal to become very vocal and demanding. Because it resonates with the throat chakra, blue lace agate can be a useful aid in calming an attention-seeking animal that expresses itself very vocally, such as a barking or whining dog or a cat that constantly miaows to gain notice.

BOJI STONE	
Healing Qualities	Aids tissue regeneration and healing Boosts energy flow and strengthens meridians Enhances attunement and co-operation between animals and humans
Indications for Use	Lack of partnership between people and animals Poor healing Rescue Animals Training problems
Chakra Resonance	Works on all chakras, especially Base.

The blackish boji stone is a rather unattractive crystal that looks like a lump of dried mud. But in its healing properties, boji stone shines and sparkles.

In a profound and inspiring way, Boji Stone helps and encourages animals and their carers to attune to one another, forming strong two-way bonds based on mutual trust, communication and respect. In this, it is similar to the FES (Californian) Flower Essence **Cosmos**. If both the animal and the carer use boji stone—perhaps the simplest way being for them both to receive regular doses of the Boji Stone essence over a period of time – it will help promote a better entente and relationship between them. Many people say of their animals: "He just doesn't seem to listen to me"; "he doesn't respond to me". And undoubtedly, animals must also often look at us and be aware of how little we understand them. Somewhere along the line, communications have broken down. If this has happened to you, boji stone may be the answer, or at least a big part of the answer, to the problem.

This very special quality of boji stone makes it an excellent training aid. Scatty animals that respond poorly to their owners' needs and commands, or appear more interested in their own affairs, can be seen to become far more responsive after use of the essence or stone. It should be considered by everyone trying to form a partnership with an animal, such as horse-riders, farmers with working dogs, trainers, military and police dog handlers and mounted police, and visually impaired people depending on guide dogs. The more intense and interdependent the relationship needs to be between the human and animal, the more precious the potential impact of boji stone energy. The list goes on: vets and veterinary nurses, animal therapists and aid workers, staff of animal rescue and rehabilitation centres, in fact, everyone in any way involved with animals would potentially see great results if they used the crystal themselves and gave it to animals in their care. Probably the most convenient way to achieve this would be for animal and human to each take 4 or 5 drops of the essence, four or five times a day for a few weeks. Treatment could, of course, carry on indefinitely without any risk or problem.

On the physical healing level, boji stone has general healing and tissue regeneration properties. It strengthens all the chakras, as well as the meridian lines that run between and connect them, sending energy around the body. Boji stone will thus contribute to and help enhance the healing of any physical ailment or injury.

CARNELIAN	
Healing Qualities	Boosts confidence and energy Enhances the sense of touch Helps mental focus and concentration Improves appetite Increases the will to live Maintains the vital force during illness Stimulates the mental and physical faculties of older animals
Indications for Use	Depression Fading life energy Lack of focus Low confidence Low energy Poor appetite Sad elderly animals Training problems Weakness during illness
Chakra Resonance	Sacral

This orange stone is an excellent healer for daydreamers and those who complain of feeling dazed and "not with it". In animal treatment, it can be used for lack of mental focus, listlessness, lack of energy both in mind and body, and the inability to concentrate the mind and maintain attention on something. As such, it is another excellent training aid and could be used in combination with **boji stone**. Its healing properties also go beyond training issues, making it worth considering for any kind of state where an animal appears to be dulled in its enthusiasm for life, lacking in "go", depressed or low in confidence. Any of these symptoms could possibly indicate an underlying state of illness, and so it would be worthwhile checking with the vet. Carnelian could then be used alongside whatever treatment was used for the illness: it would support homeopathic treatment in the quest for health, and would maintain the animal's vital force if suppressive allopathic means had to be used. Carnelian's energies also boost the appetite, which is an important benefit, as so many sick animals lose interest in food and become further depleted by lack of nutrients.

Sometimes depression and lethargy are not symptoms of disease as such, but signs of an animal losing its vital spark as it ages. Older animals, especially dogs, can become more fearful and lacking in confidence as the years pass by. They may go into themselves and become reluctant to leave the home, as they feel more protected there; thus, they fail to get the exercise they need, and this can contribute to their failing health. Carnelian is especially useful for reversing this cycle, and will help to stimulate their mental and physical faculties, encouraging more interest in play, exercise, the outdoors, food, and life in general.

Another candidate for carnelian is the old riding school horse that has been retired from service, turned out all alone in a field, and becomes depressed. When one considers how old people deteriorate when they are alone and sad, it is not so surprising that an emotionally sensitive creature like a horse can fade and give up.

Carnelian additionally has the fascinating property of enhancing the sense of touch. It is an intriguing stone to touch and play with: sometimes it feels soft, almost so soft that one fancies it could be squashed flat between finger and thumb; then other times it feels terribly hard and inflexible. Other users have reported a greater feeling of touch-sensitivity through their fingertips after handling or carrying a piece of carnelian for a while. Carrying the crystal or taking the essence could thus benefit trainers and therapists using techniques such as TTouch (Linda Tellington), Contact Learning (Julie Sellors), massage, or other hands-on therapies.

CHERRY OPAL	
Healing Qualities	Aids healing after surgery Boosts energy and vitality Cleanses the blood Helps with convalescence Speeds up tissue regeneration Supports birthing process
Indications for Use	Convalescence Fatigue and exhaustion Poor healing Post-birth recovery Post-surgical recovery Weakness
Chakra Resonance	Sacral, Crown

There is a popular belief that opals bring bad luck! However, there is no truth in this. Jacquie Burgess, in her book *Crystals for Life*, explains that this was a myth perpetrated by the diamond industry in the nineteenth century to sabotage the threat from the booming opal industry.

Cherry opal is a very useful crystal that will help any animal that has had an operation, from common routine work such as spaying and castration to serious life-saving surgery. It has the ability to speed up tissue regeneration and promote healing, and so is especially beneficial to animals (and people) that heal poorly or slowly. It is similar in this respect to **Arnica**, one of the most commonly used and well-known homeopathic remedies. For post-surgical healing, cherry opal works well when used together with **rhodolite garnet**. The two crystals will complement one another nicely: the opal helps to promote healing on the physical, material level, while the garnet's energy focuses on healing the gash in the aura, the invisible, yet very real, energy body. Also like Arnica, cherry opal additionally acts as a blood cleanser and will give a boost of energy and vitality to a convalescing animal. This double benefit makes cherry opal an invaluable part of anyone's crystal or crystal essence collection.

There are many other circumstances where cherry opal could benefit an animal. Wild animals, such as fox cubs, hedgehogs or birds, that are found lightly injured or weak and exhausted, perhaps after having strayed from their mothers, can be helped back to recovery and health, and will more quickly regain the energy they need to return to their natural environment.

Cherry opal will help, too, with an animal that has just given birth and is depleted in strength. Doses of the essence could be administered to the mother during the birthing process to ease discomfort and maintain strength. This stone will also be of benefit if surgery is necessary to help with the birth. This may happen, for instance, in cases of uterine torsion in bitches, where a caesarean section is required to save the lives of both mother and young. Giving the essence to the bitch after the event, or leaving the crystal near the affected area, will help her wounds heal quickly and cleanly. Other crystals may also be brought into use to deal with the trauma she has suffered—for instance **gold**, **moonstone**, **hematite**, and perhaps **smokey quartz** or **aventurine**.

CHRYSOPRASE	
Healing Qualities	Aids digestive system Balances female emotions Boosts fertility Calms deeply, physically and emotionally Enhances relations between the sexes Encourages emotional independence Heals separation grief Regulates hormones and seasons
Indications for Use	Difficulty conceiving Digestive problems False pregnancy Hormonal imbalances Irregular seasons Irritability May assist in treatment of anorexia Mood swings in females Nervousness Pining Separation anxiety
Chakra Resonance	Sacral, Heart

This attractive apple/avocado green stone is extremely beneficial for many problems typically suffered by females, either human or animal. We have used chrysoprase a good deal in our work with dogs, and found it very useful in stabilising manifestations of hormonal imbalances such as mood swings, anxiety and neurosis, and even one extreme case of anorexia in a bitch. This little dog was deliberately and wilfully starving herself, to the point that her health was falling apart. It only took a few days of administering the chrysoprase essence, by spray bottle and topical application, to put her back into balance and start her eating again. This dog's other related hormonal problems—a tendency to broodiness and "nesting", suggesting she was going to suffer false pregnancy—also disappeared after the treatment.

We have also conducted an experiment with a number of bitches at a rescue centre that were experiencing difficulty in coming into season, or suffering from very irregular seasons and related emotional problems—mood swings, anxiety, irritability and so on. We found that when the bitches were treated with chrysoprase essence over a period of a few weeks, those with overdue seasons suddenly went into season, and those suffering from mood swings were calmed. The cases of false pregnancy were also cleared up. **Moonstone** was also used with good results.

In acting to balance and regulate the hormones, chrysoprase can aid fertility if problems conceiving are linked to hormonal levels. Bitches and other female animals that suffer from hormone-related mood swings when in season also may not be willing to tolerate the attentions of males, which is an obvious obstacle to conception! The action of chrysoprase in smoothing out emotional fluctuations, irritability and hostility in these females is conducive to better relations between the sexes.

Chrysoprase is additionally a useful crystal for treating problems of separation anxiety in animals. Certain breeds of dog, notably the German Shepherd, are known for being one-man dogs, in other words their fidelity and love is very focused on just one person in their life. When owners go away on holiday or are even away for a weekend, these dogs can suffer from acute separation anxiety. Dogs with this tendency will benefit from chrysoprase treatment starting a few days before the separation is due to take place. Our research colleague Dr John Kaplan has found that regular use of chrysoprase essence lessens separation anxiety tendencies in dogs very noticeably. Other animals also suffer from separation anxiety, whether they have been separated from their human carers or companions of their own kind. Cats left in catteries while their owners are away may pine. (This is particularly true of oriental feline breeds such as the Siamese, whose owners frequently describe them as being more like dogs than cats in terms of their great loyalty to a single person.) Horses, too, can suffer from separation anxiety and fall into states of depression when parted from either the humans or the horses that they feel closest to. We personally have not come across cases of smaller household animals such as mice, rats and gerbils suffering from separation anxiety, but there is no reason to suppose that, on some level, they do not feel something when parted from the warm contact they enjoy with their owners.

Because it works on the heart and sacral chakras and irons out emotional problems, chrysoprase can also have a positive effect on some digestive problems, particularly if linked to nerves and neurosis in animals.

CITRINE	
Healing Qualities	Aids concentration Energises Strengthens immune system Lessens overwhelming impressions of environment on young animals Protects against radiation, stress and shock Supports newborns
Indications for Use	Diabetes Emotional or sensory overload Fatique and exhaustion Low immunity Poor concentration Radiation exposure Sudden changes Training problems Vulnerable, weak or fading newborns Wile animals in captivity
Chakra Resonance	Base, Sacral, Solar Plexus, Crown

The golden-brown or orange-white citrine is a very versatile stone, and we recommend you to have one as part of your crystal collection.

One of the key uses of citrine in animal therapy is in helping to lessen emotional or sensory overwhelm. When young animals enter the world of humans, with its noise, crowds, traffic, smells and a millions things going on at once, they need to learn how to cope with the many influences and impressions that will act on them in their new environment. Using citrine will help them adapt and get used to strange and bewildering circumstances, such as being taken out in the street and amongst large numbers of people, or to shows and events, where the sheer volume of sights, smells, sounds, could be overwhelming and exhausting for them. Mental fatigue, lack of concentration, and confusion may all affect an animal that is thus suffering from sensory overload. In helping to regulate this overload, citrine makes a useful aid to early training with young animals that may get confused and fail to understand what is required of them. (See **Using Crystals in Animal Training**.)

Animals brought from the wild to a zoo may be overwhelmed by the amount of activity and all the various experiences of their new life.

citrine would help them to regain their mental clarity and focus, and assimilate all these diverse impressions without falling into a state of mental dullness.

The idea of protection from negative outside influences that threaten to overwhelm us is crucial also for physical health. On a physical level, if the organism is overwhelmed by the actions of the world around it, this makes for a lowering of immunity to illness, to bacteria, to shock, to stress—to anything that may harm us. Citrine increases the hardiness and resistance of the physical body. As such it is a useful crystal for newborn animals, who, coming into this world, are subject to a sudden and violent change that may occasionally overwhelm them if they are not strong enough. This makes citrine another useful tool to help the condition of fading puppies and any newborn animal that is weak and struggling.

Citrine also protects from the negative effects of background radiation. People who spend time working with computers often suffer from mental sluggishness and confusion after a few hours, losing concentration and energy. They would find citrine a useful antidote to this problem, which is caused by the radiation emitted by the machine. Animals living in the home—dogs, cats, birds, rodents, fish, all of which may suffer problems—also benefit from the anti-radiation properties of citrine crystal.

CLEAR QUARTZ	
Healing Qualities	Alleviates emotional extremes Amplifies and directs energy for improved healing and immunity Cleanses and purifies the blood Enhances bioenergy of the whole system Neutralises negativity and emotional resistance to healing Protects against background radiation Reduces pain, inflammation, damaged nerves and scar tissue Used in crystal massage
Indications for Use	Blood disorders Effects of radiation Highly-strung or hysterical animals Inflammation Low immunity Pain Poor circulation Poor healing Rejection of healing aid Resistance to healing
Chakra Resonance	All chakras

The instantly recognisable, transparent clear quartz is often called the ultimate healing crystal, and it is said that, if you can only have one crystal in your collection, it should be this one. Its use in modern technology is as an amplifier and transformer of energy, and its use in healing reflects those qualities. Kirlian photography has shown that clear quartz will amplify the energy of whatever part of the body it is placed near. Regular use of clear quartz will help to enhance the bioenergy of the whole system and have a positive effect on all health by raising levels of vitality and boosting the immune system.

Clear quartz plays an important function in many crystal layouts, and placing terminated clear quartz points around a painful area often alleviates pain and inflammation. Using two quartz points, it is possible to increase the flow of energy through any blocked area: this can help poor blood circulation, repair damaged nerves and scar tissue and speed up the healing of injuries and broken bones. To do this, simply hold one point on each side of the affected area, with the points facing inwards. Keep the points in place for fifteen to twenty minutes and repeat as necessary. We use this a technique a lot to heal animals with sprains and other minor injuries. Another hands-on use of clear quartz is in crystal massage, using a crystal wand as described in **Crystal Massage.** This can be done for general healing and chakra balancing.

Clear quartz also helps cleanse and purify the blood. The treatment of serious blood diseases, such as leukaemia, has been supported by the use of clear quartz.

Clear quartz will alleviate many extreme emotional states. A cat that becomes excited to the point of hysteria when going to the vet's can be calmed by using a spray of the essence at regular intervals. The same applies to other highly strung animals, such as thoroughbreds and Arab horses, who may become too agitated to be handled, examined or shod.

Another, though rarer, situation where animals may be difficult to treat is when they appear to resist healing because of an emotional blockage. Every therapist has come across people who are "clients from Hell", who fail to attend sessions and take remedies, even when they are getting good results from the therapy. It is often said these people are "not ready" for healing. The same phenomenon is apparent in a minority of animals, who seem to understand when someone is trying to help them, and resist all attempts. We have worked with a few cases like this, the most striking being a dog who was so resistant to the crystals placed around him that he would pick them up in his mouth and throw them across the room. This dog could also, amazingly, tell the difference between a large container of drinking water with a few drops of essence in it, and the same container with just plain water, and consistently avoided the treated water. We made up an essence of clear quartz in a spray, for the owner to diffuse around the room where the dog spent time, and within a couple of days the dog began to accept crystal layouts and essences added to water. As we have said, this is a rare phenomenon, but you may come across it!

As a protection against background radiation in the home, place pieces of clear quartz on or around computer terminals, televisions, and other electrical appliances. Alternatively, animals' collars can have small crystal pieces securely fastened to them; fish tanks can have pieces immersed in them, and pieces large enough not to be swallowed can be placed in cages. Doing this can have a very positive effect on the health of pets living in rooms with such equipment. (See **Case Histories: Zabadak** and section on **Exposure to Rays and Radiation**.) But don't forget to cleanse these hard-working crystals at regular intervals.

Clear quartz energy is powerful and quite sharp. For this reason, and bearing in mind that animals are highly sensitive to crystal energy and that we should never impose it upon them against their will, some animals may find clear quartz slightly overwhelming. You will soon know if an animal does not accept the crystal, as it will struggle or walk away. If this is the case, despite clear quartz being the crystal best indicated for healing the animal's problem, it may be necessary to try **milky quartz**. Milky quartz has all the properties of clear quartz, but with a slightly softer edge that animals may find more comfortable.

COPPER	
Healing Qualities	Cleanses and purifies the system Protects from toxins Soothes stiffness and aches in joints and muscles
Indications for Use	Arthritis and rheumatism Eczema Infected wounds Radiation exposure Toxicity
Chakra Resonance	Base, Sacral, Solar Plexus, Heart

This yellowish metal reduces inflammation in tissues, which explains its use in treating arthritis and rheumatism. Many people swear by copper bracelets and bangles to aid with symptoms of pain and stiffness, but fewer people are aware that an essence of copper, either taken internally or rubbed into the affected parts of the body, can have the same effect.* This method is often more practical with animals than getting them to wear copper on their bodies, and can bring about drastic improvement in those many animals that suffer from arthritic and rheumatic complaints. Elderly horses and dogs, especially those that have had competitive and athletic pasts and may have had falls and muscle sprains (for example racehorses, showjumpers, racing Greyhounds, agility dogs) often suffer from stiffness in the joints and old "war wounds". Arthritis is also common in dogs that have been in

---

* Use only copper essences that have been prepared by reputable and expert sources. Do not make your own copper essences at home, as they may contain too high a level of the toxic material.

sufficiently exercised, been overfed and allowed to get fat. In these cases, it may be too late to reverse the physical condition simply by improving the dog's lifestyle, and copper will need to be used to help deal with the symptoms of pain and stiffness.

Arthritis is considerably less common in cats than in dogs. This may be at least partly due to the fact that the average cat spends far more time outdoors than the average family dog, and is thus freer to regulate its exercise levels. Old cats are often still very agile and athletic compared to old dogs; but if they do develop symptoms of arthritis or rheumatism, copper will help them too.

Copper is a specific remedy for the ill effects of microwave radiation as emitted by cell phones. Of course, animals don't use cell phones! But there are other ways to be affected by them. Much has been made of the dangers of "passive smoking", but in years to come the public will become more concerned about "passive cell phoning", when the adverse effects, as yet largely unknown, of standing within a certain range of a cell phone user start to become apparent. Copper will help to prevent the problem, both for animals and people. Microwave ovens also emit the same kind of radiation.

A few drops of copper essence added to a poultice or dressing will help to draw impurities and infection out of minor wounds. The ancients also used copper to treat skin conditions such as eczema, which may be related to internal toxicity as it is very much more common in the modern age of poor food, pollution and noxious conventional medicine.

EMERALD	
Healing Qualities	Boosts confidence in oversubmissive animals Calms and soothes the nerves Draws out toxins and impurities Encourages emotional independence Acts as mild laxative and cleanser
Indications for Use	Constipation Excessive submissiveness Ingestion of "nasties" Minor wounds Nervousness Poor confidence
Chakra Resonance	Heart

The striking green emerald is very useful for animals that lack in confidence and are overly submissive. This mainly applies to dogs, as their whole view of the world revolves around hierarchy and rank, and they are highly conscious of where they stand within the social group structure. An overly submissive dog will tend to roll on its back and perhaps urinate in supplication when people visit the home, as a means of saying to them *"Don't hurt me—I'm only an underling and mean no harm"*. Certain breeds of dog are much more susceptible to this than others, some of the more submissive and passive ones being Cavalier Spaniels, Greyhounds and Whippets, and Shetland Sheepdogs. Having said that, any dog may suffer from this imbalance, regardless of breed. Emerald can help these underconfident dogs to behave in a more measured and independent manner.

More broadly speaking, emerald can generally help with nerves, as a calmer for all animals suffering from emotional problems.

As a mild laxative, it can be useful as a cleanser if your animal has ingested something unpleasant (not poisonous!), and you wish to flush it through their system quickly. Among other scavengers, goats are notorious for eating everything that falls in their path, and goat-keepers looking for a mild natural laxative need look no further than emerald. It will also serve to unblock simple and non-serious cases of constipation in animals.

Emerald acts to draw out toxins and impurities from the system. It also works as an antiseptic and the essence may be added to dressings on minor wounds. Those readers who know about the Bach Flower Remedies will see a similarity between emerald and the flower essence **Crab Apple,** which works to draw out impurities and toxins (compare also to **bloodstone**).

As emerald falls into the rather arbitrary category of a precious stone and is thus quite an expensive thing to purchase, a practical way of making use of it is to buy the readymade essence. It is available from the AFEP (Alaskan Flower Essence Project) range of essences (see Appendix). We would not like to advocate using a valuable ring or brooch for crystal healing with animals—just in case they are eaten, tramped on or buried in the straw!

FLUORITE	
Healing Qualities	Boosts convalescing animals back to strength Facilitates precision training Improves assimilation of dietary nutrients Improves mental focus, co-ordination and learning Strengthens the bones and teeth
Indications for Use	Anorexia Arthritis and rheumatism Clumsiness Convalescence Low vitality Poor bone and tooth condition Poor diet assimilation Training problems
Chakra Resonance	All chakras

Fluorite can be various colours, often of a mixed purple/blue/green/yellow hue. This multicoloured fluorite is quite recognisable and distinctive.

Fluorite is a very useful crystal on both the physical and mental levels of healing. On the physical plane, one of its most important qualities is that it improves the body's assimilation of nutrients from food – specifically phosphorus, zinc, calcium, magnesium and vitamin K. Thus it is helpful for convalescing animals that have been eating less than usual during illness, helping to support and feed the system and allowing them to make the most of what they eat as they build themselves back to strength. It also plays a part in the treatment of anorexia in animals, for the same reason—to help prevent them from losing vitality while the source of the problem is dealt with.

Due to its association with calcium levels in the body, fluorite will also help strengthen bones and teeth (it is far better and healthier for this purpose than the chemical fluoride that is added to tapwater in many countries and unofficially linked to many health problems). It helps to prevent and reverse tooth decay and other bone disorders, being a prime source of fluorine—deficiency of which can be a cause of dental decay and soft bones. Fluorite especially strengthens the enamel on teeth. There is also the possibility that using this crystal or crystal essence may help alleviate arthritic and rheumatic symptoms in some animals.

On the mental/emotional level, fluorite balances the left and right sides of the brain and is extremely useful as a training aid for animals, helping them to balance their rational, thinking side with their intuitive, instinctual side. For this ability, it could be used to help further enhance such advanced animal training techniques such as TTouch, Contact Learning and the Pat Parelli Natural Horse•Man•Ship approach. (See **Using Crystals for Animal Training.**) As a sharpener of co-ordination, it will help animals that have difficulty focusing their attention, seem unable to retain lessons, or appear to be clumsy. It is a key crystal to help with the training of dressage horses, show-jumpers, agility dogs or any animal in intensive, precise training. It also helps improve the co-ordination of clumsy young animals that tend to barge into things and knock them over. (This often happens with young large-breed dogs that are growing faster than they realise!)

GOLD	
Healing Qualities	Acts as a master healer Aids recovery from illness, shock and past abuse Boosts immune system and glands Eases emotional problems and reduces stress Optimises bioelectrical functioning and tissue regeneration Promotes love, openness and trust Protects against radiation Reduces toxic levels in the body Rejuvenates and supports the entire organism Strengthens the nervous system
Indications for Use	Accidents and emergencies Anger Convalescence Depression Epilepsy (consult vet) Fear Low confidence Low immunity Paralysis Past abuse Poor healing Radiation Shock Toxicity
Chakra Resonance	Heart

Gold is considered a master healer and can help with many problems. According to Simon Lilly, author of *The Complete Illustrated Guide to Crystal Healing*:

> *Gold is excellent for balancing the functions of the brain and nervous system. It works alongside all bioelectric functions of the body, and strengthens the immune system and major glands. Gold helps to stabilise electrical functioning at cellular levels, resulting in less energy waste and the reduction of stress."*

Gold can help in the treatment of neurological conditions, especially with epilepsy, which is often the result of an imbalance of electrical discharge between the right and left brain. In stimulating a balance, gold has been known to help reduce the problem.

Gold will additionally encourage tissue regeneration in the brain and elsewhere throughout the physical body. It has been used to help alleviate nerve damage and paralysis, which can strike animals in conditions such as CDRM (Chronic Degenerative Radiculomyelopathy), which destroys the use of the hind legs in dogs, and, increasingly, in cats. It rejuvenates the heart, muscles, nervous system and skeletal structure, and aids with skin regeneration. Many in the allopathic, conventional medical world would not deny gold's ability to promote the mending and bonding of tissues throughout the whole body. It is interesting that in technology, the purity of gold makes it a perfect conductor of electricity and the top choice for faultless wiring connections. We can see from its many therapeutic uses that gold is equally a great conductor of healing bioenergy.

Gold has a far-reaching beneficial impact on the whole physical organism, boosting the immune system generally and affording extra protection against illness. It boosts the vital energy of animals convalescing after a long illness or recuperating from an accident, severe fright or trauma, and cleanses the systems of animals suffering from high toxicity after periods of drug therapy or exposure to pesticides. It also offers good protection against background radiation.

On the emotional level, animals suffering from conditions of chronic fearfulness, poor confidence, anger and hostility can be helped with gold. Gold is used in homeopathy (as the remedy **Aurum Metallicum**) to help cure severe depression and suicidal tendencies in humans. Either homeopathically or as a subtle-energy mineral essence it be used in the same way for depression in animals. Animal depression can occur for many reasons, including physical illness, and so it is a good idea to consult with the vet if your animal seems to be depressed for a long time. Outside of physical causes, however, depression is frequently seen in horses, dogs, cats and other species that have been poorly treated by previous owners. Gold will act to open the heart chakra if it has been shut as a result of maltreatment or neglect, and so any animal that has thus come to resent, mistrust and fear humans can be helped to return to a harmonious rapport with their carers and people in general.

Adding gold essence to combinations of other essences, either flower or crystal essences or blends of both, is said to have an enhancing effect on the medicinal properties of the blend. In this respect it is similar to the flower essence **Lotus** which many claim enhances other flower essences and can address a great many ills.

Like emerald and ruby, gold as a substance is highly valued in financial terms. For this reason, it is often more practical to obtain ready-made essences from suppliers. Gold nuggets are not sold in very many crystal stores!

HEMATITE	
Healing Qualities	Boosts physical vitality Cleanses the kidneys Grounds, calms and sooths Improves assimilation of iron from the diet Helps to stem bleeding Maintains emotional boundaries Strengthens the blood
Indications for Use	Anaemia Bleeding wounds Blood disorders Group panic and hysteria (especially herd animals) Kidney problems (consult vet) Lack of vitality Shocks
Chakra Resonance	Base, Sacral, Solar Plexus

This shiny silvery-black stone, which looks like a piece of dull steel when polished and tumbled, is actually vivid red inside. This gives rise to its Greek name *haematites,* relating to the blood. Indeed, hematite increases the red corpuscles in the blood and is claimed to be of use in many types of blood disorder. It makes for better usage of iron in the diet. It is in fact composed of about 70 per cent iron itself—and may be used to help treat anaemic states or conditions where vitality is lacking.

It is also an extremely good kidney cleanser. Our colleague Dr John Kaplan has had excellent results treating kidney disease in German Shepherd dogs, using a combination of hematite and **bloodstone** essences. These two crystals are also related in that they can both be used to help stem excessive bleeding from wounds and in the birthing process. With this in mind it is very interesting to note that hematite was used in ancient Egypt to treat haemorrhages.

Because it balances the lower chakras, hematite is able to have a profound "grounding" effect that will protect from what might otherwise be overwhelming shock to the system. Therefore it is useful for helping to deal with shocks, traumas and frights. Steve Johnson, maker of the Alaskan Flower and Gem Essences, writes in his book *The Essence of Healing* that hematite helps when one is

> unable to maintain one's boundaries while witnessing a
> highly-charged emotional experience; getting swept away
> by others' negative feelings; ... having difficulty containing
> one's own emotional energy, especially in groups.

In animal treatment, hematite is indicated for maintaining calm amongst a group of horses. Horses feed off one another emotionally, being herd animals and also prey animals – so if one becomes agitated, there is a tendency for the agitation to spark off a reaction through the whole group. When a group of riders are out together, perhaps hacking on the public road, just one horse taking fright at something may set off all the others. Many fatal accidents have happened this way. We would suggest that attaching a piece of hematite somewhere on the saddle, preferably low down the horse's spine so that it can resonate with the lower chakras, may help calm the horse in stressful situations while out riding. (Do not, please, put the stone between the saddle and the horse!) In more chronic situations, if the horse is very prone to losing its head and you think hematite may help, try simply giving a regular dose of the essence, several times daily over a period of time. This way the crystal could be combined with any others that seem indicated, for instance **aventurine.**

Another use is with horses is in transit. Many horses panic in trailers, and terrible incidents have occurred when horses have lost control of themselves whilst the trailer was being towed. A horse can quite easily punch a hole through even the most solid-looking aluminium trailer, and may inflict serious injuries on itself and even cause a road accident. A hematite stone placed in a trailer, or anticipatory doses of the essence several times a day for a couple of weeks or so, can have a calming effect. Hematite works well together with the flower essence **Cherry Plum** in this situation.

HERKIMER DIAMOND	
Healing Qualities	Cleanses the aura Enhances telepathic communication between people and animals Flushes toxins from body Helps assimilation of magnesium and phosphorus Releases stress Strengthens bonding and attunement
Indications for Use	Poor dietary assimilation Poor human/animal relationships Stress Toxicity
Chakra Resonance	All chakras

Herkimer diamond is a fascinating and powerful stone. Used as a pendulum for scanning over the body, (see **Using the Pendulum**) it can repair and detoxify energy fields, cleansing and restoring the aura. To accomplish this, dowse over the animal's body with the herkimer diamond pendulum, and slowly work your way from the lower chakra end upwards. Where the pendulum starts to swing in an anticlockwise motion, this is a signal that it is detecting toxicity. Where it swings clockwise, things are in balance. If the pendulum is indicating toxicity, it is possible to help release it by manually reversing the swing in the opposite direction. This process of auric cleansing also helps us flush out toxins from the physical body, and so the essence can be given to any animal that has been subjected to chemical drugs and medicines. In addition, herkimer diamond enables better dietary assimilation of phosphorus and magnesium.

One of the stone's more intriguing qualities is its reputed ability to bring out telepathic links between people and animals. This is not as obscure and otherworldly as it may sound: many people claim to be able to communicate telepathically with their pets. Dick Francis, the former jockey and best-selling author of equestrian fiction, makes many references in his books to the telepathic abilities of horses. We have come across several cases where animals and owners separated by distance seemed to be able to sense what was happening with one another, and these phenomena are often difficult to explain rationally. Rupert Sheldrake, in his book *Dogs That Know When Their Owners Are Coming Home*, investigates the uncanny ability that dogs have to sense our movements at a distance. We could speculate that animals perhaps do not need much enhancement of their telepathic abilities, and it is we who need to develop ours! Herkimer diamond offers the chance of doing this.

There is another way herkimer diamond can strengthen the bond between animal and human, which will be of particular interest to people who must leave their pets behind when they go travelling. This crystal is thought to retain a "memory": so that two pieces of herkimer diamond can be attuned to one another, simply by bringing them together. If those two pieces are then separated, no matter how far apart, it is said that the attunement remains. So attaching one piece to a pet's collar and keeping the other piece as a pendant, or even just in a pocket, allows an energy link to be maintained between you and your pet over any distance. Traditionally, the diamond was given as a keepsake to loved ones moving away, so they would never forget one another. It is a lovely idea, even if such claims cannot be proven scientifically!

Herkimer diamond is also good for releasing build-ups of stress in the body, which, if left to accumulate, may eventually filter through the layers of the dynamic organism and become physical manifestations of disease. Animals are just as likely to develop cancers and other serious illnesses as an indirect result of stress as humans are, and so it follows that a relatively stress-free life, or a releasing of inevitable stresses as they accumulate, is always going to be a potential factor in longevity.

JADEITE JADE	
Healing Qualities	Calms and soothes aggression Gives strength to newborns Helps animals settle into new environments
Indications for Use	Anger and aggression Changes of environment Eye disorders Fading puppy syndrome Past abuse Rescue animals Skin problems
Chakra Resonance	Heart

Jadeite jade is a dark green stone. The use of this crystal in treating animals has been greatly developed by Steve Johnson of AFEP and Andrea Freixida of BioFauna, who have incorporated it in essence form with **black tourmaline** in their flower/crystal essence combination **Animal Rescue Formula**. It was specifically included for its demonstrated ability to release the stresses in an animal that render it aggressive. A reality of working with animals, which is easily overlooked, is the possibility of getting hurt. Too many people place themselves in dangerous situations with highly stressed or traumatised animals out of a belief that the animal will respond to their love and care for it. The truth is that no matter how much we love and care for an animal, we will not automatically be protected from violence! The smallest dog or cat can inflict impressive injuries upon our fragile human bodies if inclined to do so, and when we come to working with larger dogs, big strong animals such as horses, let alone extremely quick and powerful animals such as apes, big cats, and so on, our own physical safety becomes more and more of an issue. One of the authors of this book, having once been attacked with astonishing force by an emotionally unstable chimpanzee that had a history of suffering at the hands of humans, knows this only too well. Animals under stress, or which have suffered abuse, are often very likely to lash out. It is not that the animal is merely "fierce", but that it is suffering, threatened and most probably half out of its mind with fear. For its ability to calm and soothe the mental states that provoke an animal to act violently, jadeite jade is a highly important crystal for anyone dealing with animals on a regular basis. Pets coming into the home from a rescue background will often benefit from it, often as part of a good, consistent training program; zoo animals or wild animals in rehabilitation will often require it as well. Another very important crystal or crystal essence for such purposes is **rose quartz**.

It should be understood that jadeite jade is not a substitute for common sense, in that it will only serve to heal aggression that stems from stress and trauma. It will not take away an animal's natural sense of self-protection, or a mother's urge to protect her young. Always exercise caution. Never impose yourself on animals. Let them come to you.

Jadeite jade additionally helps animals to settle into new surroundings, so would be very useful when a new animal is being introduced to the home. Wild animals that have been taken in for nursing or rehabilitation would all similarly benefit from this crystal or crystal essence. Probably the most striking and profound experience of coming into new surroundings, which happens to us all, is the experience of birth. Being born is obviously a necessary stage in our lives and is designed by nature to work smoothly and efficiently. But there are times when, particularly in domestic animal births, the impact of emerging into the outer world can prove an overwhelming one. This perhaps partly accounts for the condition known as "fading" that is quite often seen in puppies, giving rise to the term "fading puppy syndrome". These pups are born apparently quite sound but rapidly lose vitality and die, sometimes after just a few hours. Jadeite jade can be administered to fading pups or to ones that seem to lack vitality, by gently rubbing the essence into their skin or gums. Alternatively the essence could be given to the mother as a precautionary measure before the birth, to help the unborn pups adapt to the future stress that awaits them. This should be seen as supportive of good general regimen and care for the mother dog throughout the pregnancy.

On the physical level, jadeite jade has a more limited but still useful application. Jade water—water in which a piece of the stone has been left immersed for a little while (not a potentised essence) can help to relieve some eye disorders when dabbed on with a cotton ball. Do seek veterinary advice on eye matters. The jadeite jade essence, sponged on in solution or added to a bath, can relieve problems of itchy skin. Perhaps this function is related to the fact that anxiety and stress can become seated as eczema and psoriasis, and the underlying emotional imbalance is healed by the crystal.

LAPIS LAZULI	
Healing Qualities	Aids assimilation of vitamins and minerals Flushes toxins from the body and mind Strengthens meridians and enhances flow of energy through the body Helps many physical ailments Resonates with the respiratory system
Indications for Use	Depression Low energy Poor dietary assimilation Post-traumatic pain Respiratory problems Toxicity
Chakra Resonance	Throat, Brow

Lapis lazuli, a dappled and speckled blue/white stone, is a very powerful cleanser of both emotional and physical toxins. At the same time as it is flushing undesirable elements from the body, it allows better absorption of much needed vitamins and minerals from the diet. The combination of these properties makes lapis a useful supplement for just about any animal or human. Poor dietary assimilation, which leads to all kinds of health problems and energy deficiency in general, is the reason many people turn to vitamin and mineral supplements both for themselves and for their pets. Such supplementation should not really be necessary; a decent diet, and the ability to extract from it what we require in terms of nutrients, should be all the body needs to maintain optimum balance.

Long-term use of chemical medicines, to which virtually all people and animals are subject, overloads the body with toxins and hampers the excretory organs. Lapis will help to boost our ability to maintain a healthier chemical balance. (Ideally, intake of allopathic drugs should be kept at an absolute minimum for all living beings!)

Stress, depression and, in animals, the "sponge effect" where they pick up on the emotional imbalances and unhappiness of their human caretakers, all also act to lower vitality and physical functioning. Lapis helps to release such emotional negativity, freeing the emotions from harmful influences.

Lapis lazuli helps to strengthen the energy meridians, and so enhances the flow of energy through the body, in a similar way to **clear quartz**. This makes it a very flexible healer on many levels, and it will aid in the treatment of a wide variety of problems simply by amplifying the benefits of any other treatment used. Specifically, lapis has a particular affinity with the respiratory system and will help to clear up many ailments related to this function. It is also especially indicated for treatment of head or back pain after an injury or trauma (obviously not recommended as an outright replacement for veterinary attention, should this be required).

MALACHITE	
Healing Qualities	Breaks unwanted and compulsive patterns of behaviour Corrects left/right brain imbalances Eases pains and stiffness Grounds and balances Protects against allergens Protects from background radiation
Indications for Use	Allergies Animals in unnatural environments Arthritis and rheumatism Epilepsy (Consult vet) Obsessive behaviour Radiation Training problems Travel sickness Vertigo
Chakra Resonance	Base, Sacral, Solar Plexus, Heart

This crystal is a distinctive and beautiful green with dark green and black layers. Malachite is high in copper content, and like copper it helps to protect the body against the negative effects of background radiation from household equipment—TVs, computers, and so on—to which many animals are subjected. Animals that live in homes near high voltage power lines and electricity stations will benefit—as will the humans—from pieces of malachite left around the home, or from use of the essence.

Malachite's copper content also makes it a good remedy for helping to relieve the stiff and painful symptoms of arthritis and rheumatism. We would suggest using the essence as a daily treatment, a few drops given at regular intervals, over a period of time. These chronic complaints may take a while to ease, having taken a long while to manifest in the body. Use a commercially available, expertly prepared malachite essence that has none of the toxic copper in the liquid.

Protection is a keyword of malachite healing. The crystal's protection from outside influences extends from protection against radiation to helping the body cope with potential allergens. Allergies are basically the body's inability to cope with contact with substances that should not in themselves cause a problem. It is unnatural, for instance, that pollen should cause physical symptoms such as hayfever in humans—yet hayfever affects millions of people. Rather than trying to stamp out the symptoms of the ailment (which may give the impression of a "cure" while only serving to drive imbalances deeper into the organism) we should always be asking: WHY does the body react this way? What imbalances are being highlighted here? Malachite, working at a dynamic, energy level, rather than at a chemical level, will actually help to correct the fundamental imbalances in the whole organism that have led to the weakness of allergy.

As an aid to training, malachite has a very significant use in left/right brain balancing. (See **Using Crystals in Animal Training**.) Other uses of the crystal in animal behaviour work would include helping to break patterns of undesirable behaviour that have become compulsive, for example weaving and crib-biting in horses and compulsive digging in dogs. It would always pay, of course, to try to look into the deeper reasons for these problems occurring. Animals kept in unnatural environments will often display obsessive-compulsive behaviour, the most obvious (and heartrending) example being the caged zoo animal that will continue to pace round and round in a tight circle even after being released from the cage.

Protecting, balancing and grounding, malachite may also help in cases of travel sickness in animals. We have used it to benefit a small dog who consistently became distressed and started vomiting after just a few minutes in the car. After a week of the essence and with a piece of the stone left in the car, the dog was able to travel peacefully. Malachite will often prove useful to sufferers of vertigo (which can affect animals) and also, by balancing the left and right parts of the brain, in cases of epilepsy.

MILKY QUARTZ	
Healing Qualities	(See **Clear Quartz**)
Indications for Use	(See **Clear Quartz**)

Milky quartz, as its name would suggest, looks very much like **clear quartz** except that it is rather more opaque, pebble-like, whitish and milky-looking. In energy and healing properties it has very similar properties to clear quartz, with the difference that many practitioners find its effects to be more subtle and gentle, or as Simon and Sue Lilly write in their book *The Complete Illustrated Guide to Crystal Healing*, "softer and warmer". In contrast, clear quartz energy can be quite sharp. In rare cases, animals that are very sensitive or, perhaps, ill may not like the sharper energy of the more frequently used clear quartz. So if your animal appears to find the energy from a clear quartz treatment uncomfortable, an option is to try repeating the treatment in exactly the same way using milky quartz. The results will be just as good, but the animal will feel less overwhelmed by the power of the crystal. (See the section on **Introducing Crystals to Animals** for details on how to bring crystals into an animal's aura without distressing it.) Forcing an animal to comply with a healing treatment or repeatedly trying to use a crystal that an animal experiences as unsettling can cause the animal to dislike all crystals.

Milky quartz is a relatively minor stone in itself, but as an understudy to clear quartz it is a good and intelligent addition to a crystal collection.

MOONSTONE	
Healing Qualities	Helps mother/offspring bonding Soothes and relaxes during the birthing process Stabilises emotions Produces an overall calming effect Regulates hormone balances Resonates with all female qualities
Indications for Use	"Difficult" mothers Digestive problems Hormonal problems in females Hyperactivity Hysteria Irregular seasons Mood swings Nervousness Orphaned youngsters Stressful births
Chakra Resonance	Sacral, Solar Plexus

Moonstone is a creamy, somewhat cheesy-looking stone with a colour and luminosity that is indeed reminiscent of the moon. This partly explains its name, but moonstone also has an important affinity with the moon in its influence on the breeding cycle and hormonal fluctuations in female humans and animals. Moonstone is generally to be considered a "female" crystal. It can be used for mares, bitches and other female animals that display erratic behaviour when coming into season. Regulating hormonal imbalances, it can also help in cases where females have difficulty coming into season at all. We have experimented using combinations of moonstone and **chrysoprase**, and found that irregular hormonal cycles in bitches are rendered more even and predictable. Mood swings, upsets, neurotic and hysterical behaviour in female animals, if linked to hormone imbalance, can also be smoothed out using this crystal. Imbalances in hormone levels can also cause nervousness and hyperactivity. These emotional traits can be lessened by use of moonstone.

Another important use of moonstone is in mothering and nurturing. It may be used during the birthing process, as a calming influence to keep the situation cool and relaxed. Surrounding the mother-to-be in a moonstone layout is an excellent and practical way to help reduce the stress of the birthing process. (See the section on **The Moonstone Layout**.)

Once the birth has been accomplished, moonstone enhances the bond between a mother and her young, and so can influence "difficult" mothers to be more accepting of their newborns. It is of great use if an orphaned youngster has to be introduced to a surrogate mother. For this kind of use, try giving regular doses of the moonstone essence to the chosen mother over a period of time to form a strong bond between her and the baby. Other essences, particularly **boji stone** and **herkimer diamond**, may need to be brought into use. The youngster will also benefit from these, to help it imprint the surrogate mother as its own. Depending on the individual situation, it may be that a crystal like **ruby** or **amethyst** will also be necessary to help with the loss of the natural mother.

Moonstone is also helpful for certain digestive problems, such as flatulence.

PERIDOT	
Healing Qualities	Acts as powerful cleanser of toxins Encourages group harmony Enhances energy and vitality Provides support through pregnancy and for newborn
Indications for Use	Aggression Animals in unnatural conditions Changes in the social group Diseases of adrenal glands Fading puppy syndrome Jealousy Long periods indoors Weak life force
Chakra Resonance	Solar Plexus, Heart

Peridot is an attractive green stone. It is an excellent tonic crystal that acts to eliminate toxins from the body and enhance energy and vitality. Animals that are kept in during long periods, such as sheep and cattle that are kept inside during the winter months, would benefit from some of this crystal given as an essence in their food or water.

As a powerful booster of the life force, peridot could be used to help with the condition known as "fading puppy syndrome". This is the mysterious phenomenon where young pups that have been born apparently healthy, then begin to fade and die for no apparent medical reason. Spraying an essence of peridot around the litter could help to prevent losing them in this way. It would be a very good idea to support the bitch through pregnancy by using peridot as a tonic. A piece of the crystal could be attached to her collar, if she accepts it, or else drops of the essence could be added to each meal. Both bitch and puppies will also benefit from **Jadeite Jade**.

Peridot works on the adrenal glands and has been used in the treatment of Cushing's disease, a serious and often fatal illness. We would recommend that it should play a part alongside professional veterinary treatment in helping to treat this condition.

On the emotional level, peridot helps states of jealousy. This is common among animals, and often sparked off when new animals are brought into the home and existing members of the family feel left out by the attention that is being paid to the newcomer. This sort of problem is extremely common in horses and dogs. Such jealousy is often expressed in acts of aggression; so it is definitely worth preventing this problem developing. While peridot helps on its own to resolve jealous emotions, animal keepers must also learn to respect herd/pack hierarchy and give precedence to the leader. Failing to do this can cause serious problems. One could start giving drops of peridot essence some weeks in advance of the arrival of a newcomer, to pave the way for the changes ahead.

Many animals, especially dogs, can also become jealous of new babies, feeling left out when suddenly deprived of attention. Peridot, combined with understanding of the animal's emotions, can help to remove the risk of a cat or dog harbouring aggressive sentiments towards a child.*

PLATINUM	
Healing Qualities	Enhances group stability Reduces animals' urge to bully humans or other animals
Indications for Use	Aggression Dominance Paralysis Training problems
Chakra Resonance	All chakras

We use platinum, or white gold, for aggressive, pushy animals whose use of force is over and above the level necessary to maintain pecking order in their social groups.

Theoretically, this should occur very seldom. When left to their own devices, animals with hierarchically arranged societies such as dogs and horses manage to maintain extremely peaceful and harmonious social groups that function for the optimum safety and strength of the collective. The pack or herd instinct, so fundamental to their survival through evolution, is a very strong force in them and it is entirely for the good.

However, animals, especially when kept in unnatural environments (it happens much less in the wild) can sometimes become emotionally out of balance, the stability of the group suffers and their methods for maintaining the social position become exaggeratedly aggressive.

---

* NEVER leave an infant or young child unsupervised with a jealous dog!

This applies to many different types of animals. (See the case of the two goats **Haig and Mindy**.)

Platinum will also help with animals that boss their carers about, although this is often the fault of the carers, and the animals are only reacting normally to the circumstances that have been imposed on them. Here, things can get quite complex! The classic case of this is a dog who tries to assert his leadership over human members of the household—not because he is some kind of power-hungry, domineering tyrant, but simply because he has been given the impression that the pack leadership is not as strong as it should be and that it is up to him to assume the leadership role. This then leads to much confusion for the dog when the humans start reprimanding him for trying to take over! And the more confused the dog becomes, the more aggressive he may become. These breakdowns in understanding between human and animal obviously create enormous problems when it comes to training.

In such cases of dominance, platinum may help to reduce or mellow the dog's aggression and his drive to take on leader status in the household (as will the flower essence **Vine**). However, to cure the situation completely involves gaining an understanding of the dog's way of thinking, and a regulation of the way the household is run so that the dog is left with no false impressions about his social status. He will accept this completely if it is done correctly. John Fisher's excellent book *Think Dog* explains these matters in very clear terms and is essential reading for all dog owners.

In treating physical problems, an important use of platinum is for helping with neurological problems, particularly paralysis. Conventional medicine can offer little in the way of treatment for some forms of paralysis, and owners of animals stricken with such conditions may want to try anything they can to help. Later in this book we have included the case of Ziggie, our own German Shepherd dog who suffers from CDRM. This condition progressively paralyses the hind legs and there is no effective conventional treatment. Among other crystals, platinum has been used on Ziggie to slow down the progress of this disease, and she is still able to run on all fours despite having had CDRM for a long time. (See **Case Histories: CDRM in a German Shepherd Dog**.)

RHODOLITE GARNET	
Healing Qualities	Facilitates healing of wounds and injuries Rebalances chakras after a shock to the system Repairs damage to the aura
Indications for Use	Damage to aura Phantom limb pain Poor healing Post-surgical recovery Wounds
Chakra Resonance	Base, Sacral

Rhodolite garnet is a highly valued type of garnet. Its colour ranges from red to pale violet and it has a very long and epic history of use as a healing crystal.

A great deal of crystal knowledge came from the East many centuries ago. When crusaders invaded the Holy Land and came into contact with ancient Eastern knowledge, many of them took to wearing garnets in buckles and rings and set into sword hilts, as it was believed that this crystal could protect against injuries. We tend to write such beliefs off nowadays as superstition, scoffing at the fancies of "primitive" people. But the smirk is wiped from our faces when we come to realise that much of this ancient knowledge is still far more advanced in its understanding of healing than our modern conventional medical systems. Garnet is indeed a valuable crystal, not perhaps for protecting against injuries but certainly for helping to heal them, and this on a level that the modern doctor or veterinarian largely ignores.

The valuable quality of rhodolite garnet is its particular use in healing damage done to the non-physical energy body as a result of injuries or surgery. Any animal that has suffered a wound or undergone an operation will benefit from this crystal's ability to, as one practitioner put it to us, "sew up the gash in the aura".

The many animals that are spayed and castrated would benefit from rhodolite garnet to finish off the job of healing their injured bodies, helping to remove the invisible imprint of the wound from their system and allowing them to reconnect energetically to those parts that have been traumatised. For animals that have lost limbs in amputation, the crystal will help to rebalance the lower chakras. It has been used in cases where an amputated limb was giving pain, despite no longer being there: the phenomenon of phantom limb pain. The reason this can happen is that the unseen etheric limb is still there, and has suffered a major trauma. Kirlian photography shows the "phantom" leaf that is left behind after the material, visible leaf has been cut away from a plant. Little has been written on the subject of phantom limb pain in animals, but there is no particular reason to suppose that they should not suffer from it just as well as humans. By extension, it is probable that the tail-docking that is routine in many breeds of dog such as Rottweilers and Dobermans leaves the animal with some degree of imbalance to the energy body. This imbalance is most likely the unseen factor in many cases of chronic illness in these dogs. (We have a Rottweiler of our own, docked before we acquired him, who suffered from lower-chakra imbalance until he was put right with crystals.) rhodolite garnet will help these animals to draw up the energies that are needed to finish the job of healing in these areas. Ideally, these practices, which are carried out purely to conform to arbitrary breed standards, should be discontinued along with all other deliberate and pointless mutilation of animals' bodies.

The crystal will also facilitate healing of the physical flesh. Parts of the body that heal poorly, suffer from poor blood circulation or have not returned to normal functioning after an injury or surgery can also be helped using rhodolite garnet. A layout of three to four stones could be used, a few times weekly; an easier way would be simply to give regular daily drops of the essence to the animal until improvement began to show. The pendulum is a useful tool for monitoring the progress of healing in the energy body. Rhodolite garnet essence is made by the Alaskan Flower Essence Project and distributed all over the world.

ROSE QUARTZ	
Healing Qualities	Dissipates fears, engenders confidence and love Heals effects of past abuse Opens the heart chakra to release pent-up hatred and resentment Softens hardened traits Soothes and reduces stress and its physical manifestations
Indications for Use	Anger and aggression Animals that "bristle" Fear Muscular tension and rigidity Nervousness Past abuse or cruelty Resentment Seeing all humans as bad Stress-related asthma
Chakra Resonance	Heart, Throat

This very important and easily recognisable pinkish stone is an essential part of a crystal collection, and in animal crystal therapy it is used frequently. That this should be so is unfortunate, as rose quartz is more often than not used for animals whose past involves some kind of ill treatment at the hands of humans. Many, many animals displaying traits of distress, aggression and fear turn out to have been neglectfully, cruelly or even sadistically treated. Not surprisingly, just like human victims of torture and oppressive penal systems, the animals who have experienced this kind of life may develop serious imbalances that will manifest as extreme fear or aggression, lack of trust in others and often a closure of the heart chakra and a blocked ability to love. Many animals that are taken as being ferocious and dangerous are really just victims of abuse, reacting in the only way they know how for their own survival. A particular feature of the negative rose quartz state is railing and resentment against authority figures. For the animal that has been psychologically scarred by maltreatment at the hands of human captors, the hated authority figures are us, the humans. This does not make for very good relationships, however well intentioned we may be, and often little can be done with the animal until those scars are healed. (Animals that are too aggressive to be approached will also benefit from **jadeite jade**.)

This makes rose quartz one of the most important crystal remedies for rescued animals. These poor animals can be very successfully treated for their traumas using rose quartz either by bringing them into contact with pieces of the stone, or by administering the essence. Remember, when placing stones near animals, make sure the animal cannot swallow them! (For details on how to treat animals that may be traumatised and/or aggressive, see the section on **Using Crystals for Rescued or Abused Animals**.)

Rose quartz is often said to have a "softening" effect. Interestingly, we have seen that in animal treatment this softening also extends to the coat. Animals that are bristling with repressed emotions such as rage and fear, and are then treated with rose quartz, often develop wonderfully smooth, soft and silky coats afterwards.

Muscular tension and rigidity can easily arise from a negative rose quartz state, as too many defensive emotions are stored in the body. Nervous asthma may also result from chronic anger and tension. We treated a cat that was suffering from attacks of severe asthma triggered every time the cat felt nervous or threatened (which was quite frequently). Talking to the owner, we soon discovered that the cat had been a rescue animal, and had some kind of traumatic history about which little was known. After a very brief period on rose quartz essence, the asthma was substantially relieved and has never worsened again. In addition, the cat's whole demeanour altered; formerly nervous and suspicious, it became affectionate and devoted to its keeper.

In another case, a thoroughbred mare with a history of quite severe abuse was muscularly very rigid, particularly in the head and neck where she had allegedly been beaten by her previous owner. The negative energy stored in her muscles was enough to pass into a Bowen (hands-on healing) therapist who attended to her, and the lady suffered an agonising headache which lasted for days. The mare was very aggressive and suspicious towards humans. She received a combination essence that contained rose quartz as well as **Dandelion** flower essence (which also helps to release pent-up energies stored in the muscles) and within two days she was beginning to soften; within less than ten days the muscle tension was gone and her temperament transformed. Several months later, at time of writing, neither the physical nor the emotional problems show any sign of returning.

RUBY	
Healing Qualities	Boosts interest in life Brings confidence, light and joy Enhances concentration and mental agility Heals sense of loss, loneliness and grief Increases stamina
Indications for Use	Animals that may pine to death Bereavement and grief Depression Low confidence Low energy Poor appetite Poor concentration and mental agility Resignation Separation anxiety Training problems
Chakra Resonance	Heart

Ruby is a dark red precious stone. It is very highly prized as a jewel and expensive to purchase; for the purposes of healing the ruby essence, made by AFEP among others, is a more practical option.

A key use for ruby in animals is for those whose keepers or companions have been taken away from them. We tend to distance ourselves from animal emotions by using behavioural terms like "separation anxiety", which, though they may reasonably accurately describe the animal's state of mind, may not fully convey the depth of the animal's pain. The fact is—and we should be quite clear on this—that animals can suffer from real grief, just like people, if their human and animal friends die or go away. Like **chrysoprase**, this crystal is suitable for mother animals that show anxiety and grief when their young are taken from them or sicken and die. Other times, owners may die and animals may pass into new hands, or beloved companions may suddenly no longer be there. Horses, for instance, form intense bonds with one another, and it is not uncommon for a horse that has lived together with another for many years to suffer terrible shock and bereavement when its friend dies. Animals can go on after such an event to lose confidence and joy in life, sometimes to develop deep depression and even pine away to death themselves because they have become ambivalent about existing in their physical body. Speaking anthropomorphically, we could say these are states where the animal has given up hope, no longer cares about anything or has nothing left to live for. Disconnection from, and loss of interest in, the body often means that an animal will show no desire to eat, and may just go and lie down resignedly in a corner, as though waiting for death. When animals have seemingly lost the will to live, for example fading puppy syndrome, ruby can be used to negate apathy, rekindle the vital spark and get them interested in life again. Animals whose vitality has suffered from a spell of depression will enjoy a boost in stamina from ruby. The more extreme "ruby state" should not be allowed to drag on for any length of time, as it is a dangerous invitation for physical conditions to manifest themselves. Any inherited predisposition to cancer (cancer miasm), for instance, can rapidly become activated at a cellular level during these times of extreme low, and the animal that "was always healthy till now" suddenly, apparently out of the blue, falls terminally ill and has little resistance to the disease.

Ruby also has a use in training, in helping to sharpen focus, mental agility and concentration. (For more details, please refer to the section on **Using Crystals in Animal Training**.)

SMOKEY QUARTZ	
Healing Qualities	Grounds, calms and sedates Helps adjust to life changes Helps keep accident or trauma victims calm until the vet arrives Rapid relief from acute shock or trauma
Indications for Use	Accidents and emergencies Moving to new surroundings Nervousness Shock Stressful situations
Chakra Resonance	Base, Sacral, Solar Plexus

Smokey quartz resembles a **clear quartz** that has been stained dark grey/brown with smoke. The stone or essence will have a very rapid grounding, calming and almost a sedative effect on an animal that is suffering from acute shock or trauma. The essence is probably most useful in emergencies, to quell agitation and hysteria while waiting for veterinary assistance. The humans dealing with such fraught situations as trying to keep an injured animal still and calm will also benefit themselves from frequent drops of smokey quartz essence. As with all essences, overdosing is impossible, and so even if a whole bottle gets used up, it is of no matter. Other subtle-energy essences that could be used alongside smokey quartz in acute stress situations are **Bach Rescue Remedy** (also known as **Recovery Remedy**) and the **Alaskan Soul Support** or **Animal Rescue** combinations, which both contain crystal essences.

As time passes after the traumatic incident (accident, fright, or whatever) and the animal does not seem to have settled down— assuming it is not injured and has been properly checked by the vet— a smokey quartz layout can be of benefit for grounding and adjusting. (See **Smokey Quartz Layout**.)

In less serious situations, it can be used to calm an animal that is being taken for a routine visit to the vet or a horse that is due to be shod or seen by the horse dentist. Whilst some horses are perfectly placid and calm while being attended to by farriers and dentists, others are so nervous that the job is virtually impossible. Smokey quartz may help in many cases, but it is also worth considering other crystals if, for instance, the horse may have suffered a past trauma associated with shoeing or tooth-rasping, or, less specifically, just associated with being handled by a strange man. When a horse (or any other animal, for that matter) is afraid of people, it is nearly always men: this sadly reflects the fact that it is usually men that abuse or frighten animals. If there is this extra layer of complexity to a case of a nervous animal, perhaps consider something like **rose quartz** or a**venturine** to help the animal recover from its past trauma.

The crystal is also worth giving to animals when a change is going to take place, for example when you are moving home, or when an animal is being rehomed. Horses are moved around a great deal, and sometimes need some help to settle into new places. It is said that cats attach themselves more to places than to people, and often when owners move house, the cats are unhappy in the new environment. Sometimes they will not even let themselves be caught when the family is leaving, and have to be left behind. They sense the coming change, and become resolute and stubborn about accepting it. Try giving regular doses of smokey quartz essence for two weeks or so before moving, or for longer if it is felt to be necessary, to help the cat prepare for the change. **Jadeite jade** may also be useful in such cases, to help the cat prepare for the future stress of the upheaval.

INDEX OF COMMON ANIMAL AILMENTS AND PROBLEMS

Abuse	Aventurine Gold Jadeite Jade Rose Quartz	**Apathy**	(See Resignation)
		Appetite, poor	Carnelian Ruby
Accidents & Emergencies	Smokey Quartz	**Arthritis and rheumatism**	Amber Copper Fluorite Malachite
Adrenal Gland Problems	Peridot		
Aging animals	Amber Carnelian	**Attention-seeking (See also Jealousy)** Blue Lace Agate	
Allergies	Amber Malachite	**Behaviour problems**	**(See Training problems)**
Anaemia	Bloodstone Hematite	**Bereavement and grief**	Amethyst Ruby
Anger and Aggression	Jadeite Jade Peridot Platinum Rose Quartz	**Bites and stings**	Blue Lace Agate
		Birthing	Cherry Opal Moonstone
Animals in unnatural conditions	Malachite Peridot	**Bladder problems**	Amber
Anorexia	Chrysoprase Fluorite	**Blood disorders**	Bloodstone Cherry Opal Clear Quartz Hematite
Anxiety	(See Fear, Nervousness, Panic Attacks, Separation Anxiety, Stress)	**Bonding**	Boji Stone Herkimer Diamond Moonstone

Bones and teeth, poor	Fluorite	**Diabetes**	Citrine
Change	Citrine Jadeite Jade Peridot Smokey Quartz	**Diet assimilation, poor**	Fluorite Hematite Herkimer Diamond Lapis Lazuli
Circulation, poor	Bloodstone Clear Quartz Rhodolite Garnet	**Digestion problems**	Amber Chrysoprase Emerald Moonstone
Cleansing	**(See Toxicity)**	**Disorientation**	Amethyst
Colds	Amber	**Dominance, excessive**	Platinum
Concentration, poor	(See Training problems)	**Energy, low**	Ametrine Bloodstone Carnelian Peridot
Confidence, low	Carnelian Emerald Gold Ruby	**Epilepsy**	Gold Malachite
Constipation	Bloodstone Emerald	**Eye problems**	Blue Lace Agate Jadeite Jade
Convalescence	Bloodstone Gold Cherry Opal Fluorite	**Fading puppy syndrome**	Citrine Jadeite Jade Peridot Ruby
Cystitis	(See Bladder problems)	**False pregnancy**	Chrysoprase
Depression	Amber Ametrine Carnelian Gold Lapis Lazuli Ruby		

Fatigue and exhaustion	(See also Energy, low) Ametrine Bloodstone Cherry Opal Citrine	**Human and animal relationship problems**	(See Bonding)
Fear	Amethyst Aventurine Gold Rose Quartz	**Hyperactivity**	(See also Training Problems) Ametrine Moonstone
		Hypersexuality	Ametrine
Fertility problems	Chrysoprase Moonstone	**Hysteria**	Clear Quartz Hermatite Moonstone
Fevers	Blue Lace Agate	**Immunity, Low**	Citrine Clear Quartz Gold
Healing, poor	Amber Bloodstone Boji Stone Cherry Opal Clear Quartz Gold Rhodolite Garnet	**Infections**	Amber Copper
		Inflammation	Blue Lace Agate Clear Quartz Copper
Healing, resistance to	Clear Quartz	**Jealousy**	Peridot Rose Quartz
Heat, females in	Blue Lace Agate	**Kidney problems**	Bloodstone Hematite
Heatstroke	Bloodstone	**Laminitis**	Bloodstone
Hibernation recovery	Bloodstone	**Learning problems**	(See Training problems)
Hormonal imbalances	Black Tourmaline Chrysoprase Moonstone	**Mental focus**	(See Training problems)

Mood swings (linked to hormones)	Chrysoprase Moonstone	**Post-surgical recovery**	Cherry Opal Rhodolite Garnet
Mothering	Moonstone	**Radiation**	Black Tourmaline Citrine Clear Quartz Copper Gold Malachite
Moving	(See Change)		
Muscle strains and tensions	Black Tourmaline Rose Quartz	**Rebelliousness**	(See Training problems)
Nervousness	Ametrine Aventurine Blue Lace Agate Chrysoprase Emerald Moonstone Rose Quartz Smokey Quartz	**Resentment**	(See also Jealousy) Rose Quartz
		Resignation	Ruby
		Rescue animals	Aventurine Boji Stone Jadeite Jade
Obsessive behaviour	Malachite	**Respiratory problems**	Amber Lapis Lazuli Rose Quartz
Pain	Black Tourmaline Clear Quartz Copper Lapis Lazuli Malachite Rhodolite Garnet	**Rheumatism**	(See Arthritis and rheumatism)
		Separation anxiety	Amethyst Chrysoprase Ruby
Panic attacks	Amethyst		
Paralysis	Gold Platinum	**Shock**	Gold Smokey Quartz
Pining	Amethyst Chrysoprase Ruby	**Skeletal problems**	Black Tourmaline
Post-birth recovery	(See Birthing)	**Skin problems**	Copper Jadeite Jade

Sponge effect   Black Tourmaline
Lapis Lazuli

Stress   Ametrine
Aventurine
Black Tourmaline
Gold
Herkimer
Diamond
Rose Quartz
Smokey Quartz
(acute stress)

Submissiveness,   Emerald
excessive

Surgery   (See Post-surgical
trauma   recovery)

Teeth   (See Bones and
teeth, poor)

Toxicity   Bloodstone
Cherry Opal
Emerald
Herkimer
Diamond
Lapis Lazuli
Peridot

Training   Amethyst
problems   Ametrine
Boji Stone
Carnelian
Citrine
Fluorite
Malachite
Platinum
Ruby

Trauma   (See Abuse
Accidents and
emergencies
Post-surgical
recovery
Shock
Wounds)

Travel sickness   Malachite

Vertigo   Malachite

Weakness   (See Energy, low)

Wounds   Bloodstone
Copper
Emerald
Hermatite
Rhodolite Garnet

CRYSTAL ESSENCE COMBINATIONS

These are general essence combinations that can help if you are unsure of which crystals to use in a particular situation. They may not be fine-tuned to every animal (for instance, your rescue rabbit from a sanctuary may not be showing signs of aggression!), but generally speaking they will normally cover at least some of the problems your animal is experiencing. As you get to know your animal better in terms of crystal healing, it ought to be possible to arrive at more specific choices for it and create your own tailor-made essence combinations. However, the combinations that follow are a good starting point.

Please remember that even if an animal does not need a particular essence, no harm can be done by administering it. Like flower essences, crystal essences are self-adjusting, meaning that if one is not required for healing it will simply "bounce off" and fail to act. The animal's system will only make use of energies that are needed, and ignore those that are not. Nature is intelligent!

Experienced users may want to attempt to make their own crystal essences. The section **Liquid Crystal Essences** shows how this can be done very simply, and also provides information on some of the stones that are best left to the experts to prepare into essences. We would advise that the best method for making up these combinations is to order the individual liquid essences from a reputable source, and then combine them at home. Some dealers, such as Crystal Herbs in the UK (see **Appendix** for their address) will make combinations up to order. A reputable crystal healing practitioner may also be willing to do this for you if you are unsure about doing it yourself. But bear in mind that making up essence combinations is basically very simple and straightforward. All that is needed, apart from the required ingredient essences, is an empty 30ml dropper bottle, a little mineral or spring water and a very small amount of brandy.

Any of the following combinations could be prepared as a normal dropper-type treatment bottle, or as a spray for misting around animals that cannot be handled due to problems of shyness, fear, aggression, and so on.

1. ANIMAL REHABILITATION ESSENCE

This essence benefits any animal being rehomed from a sanctuary or rescue centre; any animal that has suffered abuse, illness, deprivation or otherwise been through a difficult time. This combination will help emotional scars to heal, allowing bonds of trust and confidence to form with the animal's new carers. Fears and aggression will be eased, and the negativity that the animal has absorbed from its past keepers will be released from its system, along with any trapped resentment against, or learned distrust of, humans. In effect, this essence will help to create a new start for the animal.

We hope that readers will not have got themselves into the situation of trying to rehome an aggressive animal. However, if this is the case, a spray bottle containing Animal Rehabilitation Essence will help to ensure that you deal with the problem in the safest way possible.

Combine equal parts:
- Amethyst
- Black Tourmaline
- Rose Quartz
- Aventurine
- Jadeite Jade

2. BIRTHING ESSENCE (MOTHER)

This essence is aimed at supporting a mother, of whatever mammalian species, through the birthing process. It helps to maintain her physical and mental energy through long periods of stress and possible discomfort. The essence will additionally help to smooth over any difficulty the mother has in bonding with her young when they emerge.

Combine equal parts:
- Bloodstone (or Hematite)
- Moonstone
- Cherry opal
- Smokey quartz

3. BIRTHING ESSENCE (YOUNG)

This essence helps newborn animals with the trauma of birth and the huge change that has come over them, boosting the vital force at this vulnerable stage and helping to guard against "fading".

Combine equal parts:
- Citrine
- Jadeite jade
- Clear quartz
- Peridot

4. DETOX ESSENCE

This essence assists in the cleansing of toxic residues of pollutants, medical drugs, such as antibiotics, and pesticides, from the physical body and would be useful after a period of illness when it has been deemed necessary to give conventional drug treatment to an animal, or after a treatment with anti-parasitic products, such as flea sprays or ear mite drops. Unfortunately nearly all animals in human care are exposed to the poisons of allopathic medicine on a far too regular basis, even for the most routine and simple complaints. This makes a detox essence such as this a very useful and necessary treatment.

Combine equal parts:
- Gold
- Malachite
- Herkimer diamond
- Clear quartz

5. ENVIRONMENTAL ESSENCE

This essence is similar in concept to Detox Essence but is specifically geared to cleansing the absorption of background radiation from the body and would be a very positive and healthy supplement for all animals that live indoors in the proximity of electrical equipment, televisions, microwaves and computers, or for animals living within harmful range of overhead high voltage wires.

Combine equal parts:
- Black Tourmaline
- Copper or Malachite
- Clear quartz
- Gold

6. TRAINING ESSENCE

Whenever an animal is in training, whether basic or advanced, this essence will help to enhance the training work. It is recommended that the essence be taken by both the trainer and the animal, which will enhance two-way communication and mutual co-operation, perhaps even a form of telepathy between the two. The essence would also help whenever it is felt that a sense of partnership is lacking between a human and animal.

Combine equal parts:
- Boji Stone
- Herkimer Diamond
- Ruby
- Fluorite
- Malachite

PART IV

Case Histories

Toby, Joanne and Cleo

Toby was an ageing terrier-type mongrel who was slowly winding down after nearly fifteen years of a happy and comfortable life with his loving owner, Joanne. Joanne had had Toby since she was a small child, and Toby was very much part of her life. He also meant a great deal to Joanne's other dog, a beautiful black Great Dane bitch called Cleo.

We came to know Toby quite well, and he had a few crystal essences himself in his last few months. When he finally passed away, we knew that Joanne would be extremely distraught, and this proved true. Joanne's grief was very acute and painful. She found it difficult to go to work in the morning; this was made even harder by the fact that she had just started training as a veterinary nurse, and often had to assist in putting pets to sleep. She suffered insomnia, wept a great deal and was generally heartbroken over the loss of little Toby.

We prepared Joanne an **amethyst** essence, and recommended she take the drops as and when needed to help with the bereavement. With such cases, essences are not intended to nullify the grief or suppress the negative emotions. They are intended to allow the grieving process to run its course in a balanced way, allowing users to cope with everyday life during the mourning process and freeing them from overattachment to the memory of the loss once the mourning process is over. Extremes of sadness and related physical symptoms are ironed out.

Joanne did not know at the time what was in the essence bottle. She followed our instructions, and found that the essence was extremely helpful in taking the edge off her sadness and allowing her to sleep at night. What she had not told us was that Cleo, her Great Dane, was also suffering considerable distress in the wake of Toby's demise. She was becoming destructive in the house, was very unsettled and beginning to manifest her stress through a dry, scurfy skin condition, which Joanne later described as similar to dandruff.

Joanne tried giving a few drops of the essence to Cleo. Within a day or so, the skin problem cleared up, the destructiveness stopped, and Cleo appeared much more settled and relaxed. Together, the dog and owner were able to come to terms with their sense of sadness and loss, and move on healthily. As this is written, Joanne is in the process of looking for a new puppy.

A Sickly Cat

While working with some dogs at an animal sanctuary, we were asked by the staff there to help with a tom cat that had been brought in to them a few weeks before. The cat was extremely lethargic and looked old and scraggy. When picked up he would not move, and he would just lie in a heap wherever he was set down. He showed no interest in anything. He was eating, but did not seem able to put on any weight. The cat had been taken to the vet, and it had been suspected that the problem was feline leukaemia. Tests proved to be negative, however, and the vet drew a blank as to what else might be wrong with him. The sanctuary were continuing to look after him, but were having trouble finding a home for him. This is a common problem, as few people wish to take on a sick-looking animal for a pet. Some of the staff at the sanctuary were convinced that the cat would soon die in any case. His condition had showed absolutely no signs of improvement since he had arrived.

The cat's past history was unknown, and our experience with rescued and abandoned animals is that it is wise to treat them for trauma, even when details are hazy. We gave the sanctuary a combination containing aventurine for such trauma. The other ingredients were **lapis lazuli,** to help the cat assimilate vitamins and minerals from his diet and hopefully gain some weight, and **bloodstone** for his general lethargy and exhaustion, and to purify the blood. Finally, there was **hematite,** also for the blood, for assimilation of iron, and to provide a lift to the cat's vital energy.

After about ten days, we received a report that the cat was up and walking about. He was eating the same, but putting on weight. The sanctuary were amazed at the change and asked us to come and have a look at him. When we visited him, the old, scraggy moggy had been transformed into a much healthier and younger-looking animal. He came up to see us, rubbed himself against our legs and ran off. Two weeks later he was rehomed.

HAIG AND MINDY

When Jackie got two young goats, a nanny and a castrated billy, from a local rescue centre, she had no idea what trouble she had invited! Haig and Mindy, as she named them, had originally been reared on a farm where they had not been well treated.

Little Mindy, the nanny, seemed to settle in immediately and was sweet and affectionate. But as soon as Haig found his feet he became, in Jackie's words, "an instant rascal and a hooligan". He started with Mindy, preventing her from reaching her food bucket. He once cut her mouth open with one of his horns, and she had to have stitches. After that, Jackie fed them in separate stalls—but this drove Haig crazy with rage and jealousy, and he would ram his head against the wall in protest. Any time Jackie tried to approach or pet Mindy, Haig would become possessive and enraged. To make matters worse, he then started taking out his frustrations on the other animals on the smallholding, injuring one of the geese and trying to stick one of the dogs with his horns. On top of which, he became an adept, seemingly unstoppable escape artist, scaling whatever sort of fence Jackie erected to keep him in. As time passed, Haig then started becoming aggressive towards humans as well, although he never injured anyone. Jackie was afraid he might attack a visitor, and at this stage she was seriously contemplating sending him back where he came from.

The first crystal treatment Haig was given was a combination essence of **peridot** (insecurity from a new experience, jealousy), **rose quartz** (past trauma, pent-up anger and resentment directed at a keeper) and **platinum** (domineering behaviour, sometimes reflecting inner insecurity). The essence was added to Haig's hard feed (goat mix) as he frequently knocked over his water when he had his tantrums. Dosage was approximately 12 to 15 drops a day, given in two meals.

In three days after starting treatment, Haig began to show signs of mellowing. Where previously he often would not even let Mindy graze near him, he now suddenly seemed content to let her be. He also stopped chasing geese, hens and dogs that dared to wander near him. On the fourth day, Jackie experimented with feeding them their hard feed together, and there was no aggression. Haig was generally more relaxed-looking, and less interested in trying to scale the fences. After ten days, all aggression, tantrums and escaping had ceased. Haig's coat, which had always been wiry and coarse, also seemed to have softened and was silkier.

Jackie kept up the dosage until the bottle was empty (at around three weeks), and although Haig seemed to have been cured of his undesirable behaviour, she was concerned that he would revert back now that he was off the treatment. We recommended that she buy a lump of rose quartz (that was too large for a goat to try to eat!) and to keep it in his stall, every so often cleansing and charging it.

At the last report, Haig was still behaving well and is apparently very attached to his lump of crystal.

ZABADAK

Zabadak is a large green parrot who, last year, began to fall ill. He was listless and depressed-looking, stopped talking to his owners and started losing his feathers. He was taken to the vet for a check-up, but nothing physically wrong could be detected. The vet could only think to place Zabadak on a course of antibiotics.

These did nothing to ease his condition; in fact, he just seemed to be getting worse. His appetite suffered, and he would spend his days sitting still on his perch, looking very miserable and forlorn. Where before he liked to have a fly around the room from time to time, now he did not respond to being freed.

With veterinary permission, we were invited to call round and see if there was anything we could do for Zabadak. The first thing we noticed was that the bird's cage, though perfectly spacious and comfortable for a parrot of his size, was poorly situated right next to two computers and a lot of electrical equipment, including a microwave oven. Animals (and humans!) suffer when exposed to constant levels of background radiation in the home. This phenomenon is often undiagnosed, but may contribute to many chronic ailments suffered by all of us. It seemed to us that this was a large part, at least, of what was ailing the parrot.

The room Zabadak was in was being used as a home office, which doubled as a kitchen, living room and bedroom as the rest of the house was being renovated. Zabadak's normal place was in the dining-room, a much more healthy environment for him – but as the renovation was due to take a long time, he and his owners were all forcibly confined to this room. As a compromise, the cage was re-situated farther away from the electrical equipment, although not far enough for our liking!

We made up a combination of **gold**, **lapis lazuli**, **herkimer diamond** and **malachite,** in a spray bottle. This combination has been used successfully to cleanse the negative effects of conventional medicine, pesticides and low-level radiation from the physical body.

Malachite is one of the chief remedies for background radiation. The combination was to be sprayed in the air, all around the room to benefit not just the bird but also the room's human occupants (who, it turned out, both felt they had been suffering more colds and coughs in the six months since they started working, living and sleeping in their home office). We also suggested that they place crystals, either **clear quartz** pieces or **black tourmaline,** on or around the computers.

After about three weeks, Zabadak began to perk up noticeably. His appetite returned, and his owners began putting a few drops of the essences into his food dish. His plumage improved, and he began to fly around the room again when released from the cage.

We went to visit him some time later, and when we came into the office the parrot was perched on top of a bookcase. He saw us, came flapping down, perched on Gael's shoulder and screeched, right in her ear:

"ZABADAAAAK!"

It is worth mentioning that, after some weeks, the owners also began to feel more energised, and have been less prone to colds and infections since the crystals and crystal essences were introduced to the room.

Jenny the Hen

Jenny, or "the Jen Hen", is our little Bantam hen. She lives happily within our little flock of Rhode Island Reds, firmly at the bottom of the pecking order but generally content with her lot in life and a happy, friendly, sociable little bird. At feeding time and when they are foraging, the big reds normally only impose themselves on her with just enough force to maintain her at the bottom of the flock hierarchy. But a few months ago we heard a noisy squawking from the yard, and looked out in time to see one of the bigger hens standing on Jenny's back, attacking her quite viciously and tearing at her head. Before we could intervene, the attacker had flapped away, leaving Jenny dazed and bleeding.

We never discovered what the fight had been about—probably a dispute over a worm! But from the moment of the attack, Jenny fell rapidly into a state of what can only be described as depression. Her wounds were not serious and healed quickly, but she seemed to have lost interest in anything. She would disappear for hours, avoiding all the hens like the plague, not coming when the others were being fed, and we would find her sitting rock still under bushes. One time she was sitting in long grass and narrowly avoided being shredded by the lawnmower! She did not move or run away at the mower's approach. She stopped laying, as we could tell by the sudden lack of little white bantam eggs in her nesting box. We checked to see if she might be eggbound, as can happen with hens, but this was not the case.

We decided to try and make her better by using crystals, and settled on **hematite** for its revitalising and stimulating properties and ability to calm and soothe; **ruby** for apathy and listlessness; and **smokey quartz** for the acute trauma she had experienced in being attacked. A terminated piece of smokey quartz was placed in her nesting box. We then made up a spray bottle with hematite and ruby essence, and sprayed it round her whenever we found her sitting still, several times a day for three days. We were also able, because she was so passive, to massage the essence combination into her feathers.

On the fourth morning there was a little white egg in Jenny's nesting box! She was nowhere to be seen, and we went hunting for her. We found her out rooting in the woods with some of the red hens, apparently back to her normal self. We stopped with the crystals at this point, apart from the Smokey Quartz which was left in the nest for a few days longer. Jenny appeared to have completely recovered from the trauma, and has never needed any further treatment. Luckily, she has managed to avoid getting into any more fights, too.

A Grumpy Llama

Jack the llama, one of a small herd living in Wales, had injured his leg while out in the field. The leg was cut at the knee, possibly lacerated by barbed wire, but the owners, Owen and Rachel, deemed it not serious enough to warrant calling out the vet. They gave the cut a cursory cleaning and left it at that. Unfortunately, the cut became infected and within a few days Jack was sporting a large and painful abscess. The vet had to be called now, and Jack was given a cleaning up and a course of antibiotics. The vet left instructions that Jack should be restricted to his stall for a while, that the wound had to be kept clean and the dressing changed regularly. But Jack, who was in a little pain and not a very good patient, did not take kindly to being handled and having his leg tampered with. Every time the owners approached him in the stall he would spit, kick and try to bite them. This behaviour was making it very hard to change the dressing properly. They were both bitten at least twice, received a few painful kicks and were trying to do the job so fast in their fear of the llama that they were concerned they weren't cleaning the wound well enough.

Rachel contacted us, asking if we could make up something "alternative" to make Jack more approachable. She said he had always tended to be grumpy and bad-tempered, but never openly aggressive before.

We wanted to try crystals with Jack, but thought that Rachel and Owen would find the idea too strange and so decided not to be too open, at least initially, about what we were giving them! We let them believe that the remedy we gave them was some herbal mixture, when, in fact, it contained nothing but crystal essences: **jadeite jade** for aggression and bad temper; **blue lace agate** for aggression and also for any heat and inflammation in the wound; **boji stone** for tissue regeneration and healing, and to promote greater co-operation with the owners; and **emerald** as an antiseptic.

The essences were in a spray bottle, which we suggested could be used to mist around inside Jack's stall at regular intervals through the day. It could also be used to moisten the dressing and keep the wound clean and cool.

The essences were posted first class on a Tuesday morning, and on Wednesday evening we received a phone call. Rachel and Owen had been taking turns to mist the essences around Jack's stall, as we had said to do, but had been rather sceptical about the chances of anything happening (we wondered how much more so they would have been if they had known what was really in the bottle!). Then, later in the day when they had gone in to change the dressing, anticipating another round of aggression and biting, they were in for a surprise. Jack was suddenly much more docile. He still snorted a little, shifted about and lifted his feet semi-threateningly while they were changing his dressing, but he let them get on with it with no acts of aggression. They were able to give the wound a thorough cleaning for the first time since the vet had been, took the time to spray some of the essence on the fresh dressing and made a good job of it.

When they returned the next day to inspect the dressing, Jack was now completely quiet. The wound itself was cool to the touch and healing remarkably fast.

Within two more days, Jack was freed from his stall and could run free in the field with no need for a bandage on his leg.

An interesting outcome of this case concerned Owen himself. Rachel called us a few weeks later to say that since the episode with Jack's leg, Owen had undergone a strange and unexpected personality change! Owen had always been a "road rager". Previously, he had always been impatient either when driving or as a passenger, shouting at tractors in the narrow lanes for holding him back, always quick to honk his horn and pick a fight at the traffic lights if the car in front failed to pull away fast enough. Since using the spray for Jack, Owen was suddenly much more laid back, less gruff with people and generally more relaxed and easy-going. Rachel asked if she could buy any more of the "herbs" for him!

MARTHA THE SHEEP

Martha is a pet sheep who thinks she is a dog! She was brought up with a pack of collies since birth, and has spent her life running and chasing with the dogs. One day, Martha was playing with her canine companions when she got a little too carried away and ran out of the field straight in front of a car. The driver managed to stop, but not before he had caught her with the front wing and sent her flying into the ditch. Martha suffered a broken leg and many bruises and cuts. She was stitched up and her leg set by the vet, and for a month afterwards she was on homeopathic Arnica. But the sheep never seemed the same after the accident. She had stopped playing with the dogs and would stand around looking rather sad. At night she would bleat nervously, and as she slept in the house she was keeping everyone awake. Sometimes she would only sleep if Katie, her owner, came down and slept in the kitchen with her. Katie had tried homeopathy, herbal remedies and Reiki, and wondered if some crystal therapy might not help her. She also felt that the broken leg had not healed quite right. It seemed slightly stiff. Perhaps it was causing pain?

We decided to try some layout work with Martha, and we chose **amethyst** initially for her stress and night fears. Her bed was in front of the kitchen fire, and it was a simple matter to tempt her in with a snack and get her to lie down. Running our hands over the prone sheep, it was possible to feel tension coming from her, as though she were unable to relax fully. Once she was still, we set an eight-piece amethyst layout around her bed: a piece at the head and foot of the bed and three opposed pairs running the length of her body. (See **Amethyst Layout**.) We had half-expected Martha to get up and walk away from the crystals, but she accepted them immediately and lay happily for half an hour in the layout, until we came over and removed the stones. During that time, Martha seemed to become very relaxed, more so than Katie had seen her since the accident. Martha slept for two hours after the layout. Katie was impressed, and we marked the tiled floor with some chalk to show her where she could lay the Amethyst pieces herself. We asked for the layout to be repeated every night for half an hour, over seven days.

From the very first layout, Martha was noticeably more relaxed at night and stopped bleating nervously. She was sleeping soundly, and Katie even had to wake her up when she came down in the morning. During the day, Martha seemed to "come out of herself" a little.

Next we decided to try some crystal massage on the leg, using a **clear quartz** wand. The procedure we followed was as described in the section on **Crystal Massage** in this book: starting at the tail end of the sheep with the rounded end of the wand pointing inwards, we worked our way up the animal's body, paying special attention to the injured leg. As the wand passed through that area, it was possible to feel the blockage of energy where the wand "stuck". After twenty minutes, the wand seemed to pass more smoothly through the area, and then it was time to invert the wand and work back down the sheep's body, bringing the session to a close.

The massage was carried out three times a week for three weeks. We were now one month into the treatment, and the change in Martha was very positive. The stiffness in the leg seemed all but cured and she was now beginning to show a desire to run with the dogs again. We thought perhaps that what was stopping her was a fear left over from the accident trauma, and so for one week Martha was given a mixture of crystal essences, four times a day. The bottle contained aventurine for the trauma of being hit by the car, amethyst for general fears and anxiety, and rhodolite garnet for the damage to the aura caused by the accident and the surgery. The essence mixture seemed to finish the job of Martha's healing, taking away her hesitation and nervousness about playing with the dogs again. At the end of the fifth week of treatment she was completely restored to her old self, and has been well and happy ever since.

CDRM IN A GERMAN SHEPHERD DOG

Chronic Degenerative Radiculomyelopathy is a very serious, debilitating condition of the hind quarters that commonly affects German Shepherd dogs but is increasingly seen in other breeds. It is a creeping paralysis that eventually leads to the complete loss of control of the hind legs, tail, and often bowel and bladder. It is painless, but there is no effective conventional veterinary treatment and once diagnosed the dog is more or less condemned to euthanasia within a short time.

This is the case of our own eight-year-old German Shepherd, Ziggie. Fifteen months ago, we noticed she was limping with her right hind leg. We initially thought this was just another in a long line of injuries, as Ziggie has been rushing about madly her whole life and suffered the occasional sprain. We gave her **Arnica** in 200c and then 1M homeopathic potencies, but this did not appear to have any effect. After ten days when Ziggie was still limping, she was taken to the vet and CDRM was diagnosed. The conventional treatment we were offered was a course of anabolic steroids, which we did not want to use as they are generally ineffective in such cases and can additionally cause a range of side-effects. We did have a few acupuncture sessions with Ziggie, and while these undoubtedly did some good, there was little in the way of visible results.

At her worst, Ziggie has been very badly affected by the condition. If we picked up her right foot and moved it back, it would remain in that position as though she had no control over it. Her tail was very dead-looking, hanging limply down between her back legs. And at one stage it looked as though she was beginning to lose bowel control; and she was leaking urine at times. Some days she could hardly walk, and would collapse if she turned or if any lateral force was applied through the hind legs. These dramatic symptoms appeared with frightening speed, within days. Indeed, this condition can destroy dogs within a short time of onset/diagnosis.

Ziggie's treatment has been with a combination of homeopathy and crystals. Her homeopathic remedies have been many—**Conium, Plumbum Metallicum, Hypericum** to name but four, with potencies starting low and climbing into the higher ranges. There is no doubt that these remedies have done a great deal, but there is equally no doubt that the crystals have contributed at least 50 per cent, if not more, to her progress.

Every day, Ziggie gets a **clear quartz** triangle layout around her back feet and legs. A **herkimer diamond** is placed near the quartzes to amplify the energy and carry out healing in its own right. A **smokey**

quartz is placed at the base chakra, and a **carnelian** at the sacral near her spine. In addition she is given essences of **gold** and **platinum,** both of which are particularly indicated for neurological disorders and paralysis, and **rhodolite garnet** to help replace energy to damaged and non-functioning parts.

After adding the crystal therapy to the homeopathy, we soon began to notice some radical changes. The strength seemed to return to Ziggie's legs, and she was able to walk and run across the fields with us as she used to. Carrying out the "leg test", where we placed the paralysed foot a few inches back to determine her level of control over it, we were pleasantly surprised that the foot would immediately jerk back into place when released. Where before her confidence was completely shot and she was unwilling to leave the house, now suddenly we were seeing her pride and independence returning, and she was spending time outside on her own again. Her bowel and bladder control returned and there is now zero incontinence. Most spectacular of all, the dead and limp tail started wagging again, as though it had suddenly come back to life. Her tail is more or less back to normal as this is written. Yesterday, after fourteen months of CDRM, Ziggie ran full-pelt for two hundred yards across a grassy field and kept pace with a fit three-year-old Rottweiler. No mean feat for a paralysed dog!

We have found through experiment that if the crystal therapy side of Ziggie's treatment is stopped for a day or two, she begins to deteriorate again. This shows that, although the crystals are really only palliating her condition, allowing temporary relief from the symptoms, they are doing so in a very powerful way that is additionally free from any side-effects.

We are not claiming a cure for this disease, but we do believe that the crystals are doing a great deal to slow down the degeneration that goes with CDRM. If this adds a few months or another year to Ziggie's life, and she is allowed some extra quality time in this way, it is a triumph for natural therapy. We would hope that in the future, many other dogs in the same predicament can benefit from this kind of healing and be spared, for a while at least, from euthanasia.

The "Haunted House"

A couple living not far from us contacted us to ask for help with their dog, Bobby, who was showing signs of agitation and hyperactivity.
When we visited the house, we saw that this four-year-old Labrador was definitely being stressed by something. The owners, Diane and Kevin, said that since moving to their new home about nine months ago, Bobby had taken to obsessive digging in the garden, whining, pacing up and down and chewing furniture. At times his behaviour was uncontrollable, and this marked a great change from his previous self, as before they moved house he had been placid, calm and well behaved.

As Diane was filling in the details, we were assuming that this was a fairly ordinary case of a hyperactive dog, perhaps related to diet, poor training, family stresses or other factors, notably the change of environment (although it seemed odd that the dog was not settled after nine months). We spent some time sitting with Diane and Kevin in their large country kitchen, asking questions about Bobby and drinking mugs of hot chocolate as the fire crackled and the November mist darkened outside.

Gael was explaining about some of the essences we might try to use and the training techniques and dietary changes that would back them up, when a look seemed to pass between Diane and Kevin. It was as if they were saying to one another: "Shall we tell them?" Then Diane leaned across the table and whispered: *"Do you believe in ghosts?"*

We didn't quite know what to say, and Diane went on. She explained that they believed, though they had been reluctant to tell us until they had sounded us out, that part of their property was haunted, and this was the root of the dog's problem. She invited us to come with her and see what we thought. We followed her outside, across the yard to a gate. Through the gate, we followed a path for about two hundred yards, until we came to a converted barn. This was Kevin's office that doubled as a shop and showroom for their home business. Kevin spent much of his time in there, and Bobby would lie at his feet. They were convinced that "something" in that office was affecting the dog.

When we walked in, Gael shivered. Diane noticed and said, "See, you've felt it too. Feel that radiator." The radiator was on full blast, burning our fingers. Yet the room was strangely cold and very uninviting despite being tastefully and attractively decorated. Kevin said he had to wear a jacket all the time he was in there. But it wasn't just the temperature. He also felt his energy and emotions affected by the room, as though he were being drained, and he had toyed with the idea of going on antidepressants. He had noticed that when Bobby spent less time in there, at the weekend when the office was shut, he seemed less hyper, but would revert back on Monday evening after a few hours in the place. They had tried shutting him out, but he wanted to be with Kevin and would whine and scratch at the door. They were desperate for help, and were going to call in a priest to bless the office if nothing else worked.

What Kevin and Diane didn't know was that this wasn't the first time we had come across a problem like this. The area they live in is full of tall electrical pylons—in fact, we still call it "pylon valley"—and it seems that many people there suffer from associated problems. One of these is negative energy in rooms, occasionally taken as a supernatural phenomenon. We had noticed as we drove into the property that it was very much in the pylon zone, although we had not made the connection with Bobby's problem. Now, stepping outside, we saw by torchlight that a large pylon loomed up behind the trees on the hill above the office, half-hidden from view, the high voltage wires passing directly over the roof of the building. We told the couple that we thought this might be the answer, and that many people believe that high voltage electricity supplies create negative electromagnetic fields that are unsettling and not particularly healthy to those living in their midst.

So having been called in to treat a dog, we were now suddenly treating a building! We returned the next weekend with four pieces of terminated **clear quartz,** a medium-sized **amethyst** cluster, and a spray bottle containing **black tourmaline** essence. Diane and Kevin looked on slightly bewildered as we sprayed the black tourmaline essence all around the room. A piece of clear quartz was placed in each corner of the room with the points facing outwards to direct the energy away, and the piece of amethyst was placed on a table in the middle of the room to help create a pleasant and relaxing ambience. We left instructions on how to cleanse the crystals, recommending that this should be done frequently, and asked Kevin and Diane to keep us informed of any changes.

Changes to the room's energy began to happen within twenty-four hours. On Monday afternoon a regular customer commented: "What have you done in here? It's a lot warmer and cosier." Kevin and Diane noticed that the energy in the room seemed to have shifted, so that first the outside edges of the room felt warmer, then over the course of the next two days this feeling spread towards the centre of the room, until the whole place felt very different. They even turned the heating down.

Our plan had been that if the dog's nervous state did not improve by rebalancing the energy in the office, we would have to start looking into other factors. We would have tried treating Bobby for the change of environment, and would have given him essence of **smokey quartz** to start with. But this was not necessary. By Wednesday, Bobby was considerably less agitated, no longer showing any signs of hyperactive behaviour.

We heard no more from Bobby's owners until Christmas time, when we received a card from them. The office was still normal, they were cleansing their crystals regularly, and best of all, Bobby was back to his old self. In this case, the "patient" never received a single dose! Later on, we suggested that everyone in the family take occasional doses of our Environmental Essence combination. (See **Crystal Essence Combinations**.)

PART V

Appendix

CRYSTALS AND CHAKRAS

Crystals that are particularly associated with each chakra, and are especially suggested for chakra healing and layouts, are marked in **bold**.

Chakra	Crystals
Base	**Black Tourmaline**; **Bloodstone**; **Boji Stone**; Citrine; Clear Quartz; Copper; Fluorite; **Hematite**; Herkimer Diamond; Malachite; Platinum; Rhodolite Garnet; **Smokey Quartz**
Sacral	Boji Stone, **Carnelian**; Cherry Opal; Chrysoprase; **Citrine**; Clear Quartz; Copper; Fluorite; Hematite; Herkimer Diamond; Malachite; **Moonstone**; Platinum; Rhodolite Garnet; Smokey Quartz
Solar Plexus	**Amber**; Ametrine; Boji Stone; **Citrine**; Clear Quartz; Copper; Fluorite; Hematite; Herkimer Diamond; Malachite; Moonstone; Peridot; Platinum; Smokey Quartz
Heart	**Aventurine**; Bloodstone; Boji Stone; **Chrysoprase**; Clear Quartz; Copper; Emerald; Fluorite; Gold; Herkimer Diamond; **Jadeite Jade**; **Malachite**; Peridot; Platinum; **Rose Quartz**; Ruby
Throat	Amber; **Blue Lace Agate**; Boji Stone; Clear Quartz; Fluorite; Herkimer Diamond; **Lapis Lazuli**; Platinum; Rose Quartz
Brow	**Amethyst**; Ametrine; Boji Stone; Clear Quartz; **Fluorite**; Herkimer Diamond; **Lapis Lazuli**; Platinum
Crown	**Amethyst**; **Ametrine**; Boji Stone; Cherry Opal; Citrine; Clear Quartz; Fluorite; **Herkimer Diamond**; **Platinum**

WHERE TO OBTAIN CRYSTALS AND CRYSTAL ESSENCES

For Crystals Themselves: Hunt around! Many markets will have stalls that sell pieces at a good price, and little crystal or New Age shops are tucked away in every town. If possible, get to see and handle stones before you buy them. Failing that, there are many reputable dealers of crystals who can supply by mail order.

USA: **Mystic Merchant**, Sennes, Alabama 36575
Tel: 1 251 645 9081
Email: mystic@mysticmerchant.com
Website: www.mysticmerchant.com

          Multistone International, 135 South Holliday St., Strasburg, VA 22651
Tel: 1 540 465 8777
Email: msiinc@shentel.net
Website: www.multistoneintl.com

UK: **Isis**, 1 Market Place, St Albans, Herts, AL3 5DR
Tel: 01727 866 720

          Opie Gems, Paradise Valley, Llangynin, St Clears, Carmarthen SA33 4JY
Tel: 01994 230212
Email: sales@opiegems.demon.co.uk

          The Rainbow Crystal Shoppe (Online crystal supplier)
Website: www.rainbowcrystalshoppe.com

For Crystal Essences contact:

USA: **Alaskan Flower Essence Project**, P.O. Box 1369, Homer, Alaska 99603
Website: www.alaskanessences.com

          Pegasus Products, P.O. Box 228, Boulder, CO 80306
Tel: 1 800 527 6104

Flower Essence Pharmacy, 6265 Barlow Street, West Linn, OR 97068
Tel: 1 800 343 8693 or 1 503 650 6015
Website (crystal essences link):
www.floweressences.com/Gems.html
The Flower Essence Pharmacy is a major centre for all manner of dynamic essences in the USA, stocking among many others the Alaskan, Pacific, Pegasus, Renascent and Siskiyou ranges of crystal essences.

UK: **The International Flower Essence Repertoire** (IFER), The Living Tree, Milland, Nr. Liphook, Hants GU40 7JS
Tel: 01428 741572
Email: flower@atlas.co.uk
IFER stock all of the Alaskan crystal essences mentioned in this book.

Crystal Herbs, D, Gilray Road, Diss, Norfolk IP22 4EU
Tel: 01379 642374
Email: Information@crystalherbs.com
Website: www.crystalherbs.com

Pencraig Essences
Tel: 01267 281761
Email: flower_essences@uku.co.uk
Producers of individual and combination crystal essences for animals, including the combinations described in this book.

Elsewhere Overseas:

Rock and Gem Shop, London Arcade, Durban, South Africa

The Wellstead, 1 Wellington Avenue, Wynberg, Cape 7300, South Africa

The Rock Shop, Arcade 83, Shop 4, 83 Longueville Road, Lane Cove, Sydney, NW 2066, Australia

Gem Rock and Minerals, 52 Upper Queen Street, Auckland, New Zealand

FURTHER READING

Bailey, Gwen. *The Rescue Dog.* Hamlyn, 1995.

Bower, John and David Youngs. *The Dog Owner's Veterinary Handbook.* Crowood Press Ltd, 1989.

Burgess, Jacquie. *Crystals for Life.* New Leaf Publications, 2000.

Chandu, Jack F. *The Pendulum Book.* C.W. Daniel, 1990.

Chase, P.L. and J. Pawlik. *The Newcastle Guide to Healing with Gemstones.* Newcastle Publishing Co. Inc., 1989.

Davidson, John. *Radiation—What It Is, How It Affects Us and What We Can Do About It.* C.W Daniel, 1986.

Edwards, Hartley. *A Horseman's Guide.* Hamlyn, 1969.

Fisher, John. *Think Dog!.* Blandford, 1995.

Graham, Helen. *Healing with Colour.* Gill & Macmillan, 1996.

Gurudas, *Gem Elixirs and Vibrational Healing Vol. I & II.* Cassandra Press, 1989.

Harrison, Stephanie and Tim. *Crystal Therapy.* Element Books, 2000.

Johnson, Steve. *The Essence of Healing.* Alaskan Flower Essence Project, 2000.

Keyte, Geoffrey. *The Healing Crystal.* Cassells, 1989.

Keyte, Geoffrey. *The Mystical Crystal.* C.W. Daniels, 1996 (Revised Edition).

Lilly, Simon. *The Complete Illustrated Guide to Crystal Healing.* Element Books, 2000.

Lilly, Sue and Simon. *Crystal Doorways.* Capal Bann Publishing, 1997.

Parelli, Pat. *Natural Horse•Man•Ship* (Educational Program).

Pitcairn, Richard H. and Susan Hubble Pitcairn. *Natural Health for Dogs and Cats.* Prion, 1989.

Rogerson, John. *Training your Best Friend.* Stanley Paul, 1993.

Scott, Martin J. and Gael Mariani. *Bach Flower Remedies for Horses and Riders.* Kenilworth Press, 2000.

Scott, Martin J. and Gael Mariani. *Dogs Misbehaving—Solving Problem Behaviour with Bach Flower and Other Remedies.* Kenilworth Press, 2001.

Sheldrake, Marianna. *The Crystal Healer*. C.W. Daniel, 1999.

Sheldrake, Rupert. *Dogs That Know When Their Owners Are Coming Home*. Arrow Books, 2000.

Tansley, David V. *Chakras, Rays and Radionics*. C.W. Daniel, 1996.

Verspoor, Rudolf with Steven Decker. *Homeopathy Re-Examined*. Hahnemann Center for Heilkunst, 1999.

White, Ian. *Australian Bush Flower Essences*. Findhorn Press, 1993.

Whitmont, Edward C. *The Alchemy of Healing*. North Atlantic Books, 1993.

ORGANISATIONS AND EDUCATION

S.A.F.E.R. (Society for Animal Flower Essence Research) is an international society for pet owners, therapists and anyone interested in using flower essences and crystal essences for enhancing animal health. S.A.F.E.R. produces a quarterly newsletter, examining the effects of individual essences and new combinations, as well as presenting accounts of case histories and articles written by members. S.A.F.E.R.'s membership comprises interested owners and practitioners from many countries of the world, including some of the top names in crystal, flower essence and homeopathic therapy.
S.A.F.E.R., Pengraig Fach, Near Blaenycoed, Carmarthen, Carms SA33 6EU
E-mail: flower_essences@uku.co.uk

The Animal Care College, a distance learning education centre based in Ascot, Berkshire, UK, is now offering an introductory course in holistic therapies for pet owners that includes a unit on crystal healing. By following this course, animal carers will be in direct correspondence with their specialist tutors, deepening their understanding of natural medicine and being guided as they learn. ACC courses are either accredited or in the process of becoming accredited, through the Open College Network. For further information, contact: The Registrar, The Animal Care College, Ascot House, Ascot, Berkshire, SL5 7JG, UK.
Tel: 01344 628269
E-mail: Admin@rtc-associates.freeserve.co.uk
Website: www.animalcarecollege.co.uk